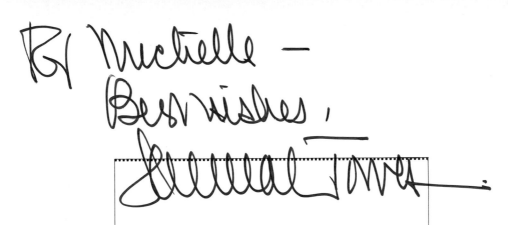

To Michelle —
Best wishes,
Jeremiah Tower

Stars Desserts

by
Emily Luchetti

Foreword by
Jeremiah Tower

Photography by
Michael Lamotte

Design by
Michael Mabry

Prop Styling by
Sara Slavin

HarperPerennial
A Division of HarperCollins Publishers

To Jeremiah, who created Stars
and made this book possible

A hardcover edition of this book
was published in 1991 by HarperCollins
Publishers.

Stars Desserts

Copyright © 1991 by Emily Luchetti

HarperCollins books may be purchased for educational,
business, or sales promotional use. For information
please write: Special Markets Department,
HarperCollins Publishers, Inc., 10 East 53rd Street,
New York, NY 10022.

First HarperPerennial edition published 1993.

The Library of Congress has catalogued the hardcover
edition as follows:

Luchetti, Emily 1957–
    Stars Desserts
    Emily Luchetti: foreword by Jeremiah Tower—1st ed.
        p.   cm.
    Includes index.
    ISBN 0-06-016688-6
    1. Desserts. 2. Stars (Restaurant: San Francisco, Calif.).
I. Title.
TX773.L79 1991   641.8′6-dc20   90-56386

ISBN 0-06-092218-4 (pbk.)

93 94 95 96 97 DT/RRD 10 9 8 7 6 5 4 3 2 1

Savarin with
Grand Marnier Sabayon
and Mixed Berries
(see page 73)

Table *of* Contents

Foreword *by* Jeremiah Tower
8

Introduction
10

Custards, Puddings, *and* Trifles
14

Hot Desserts
44

Fruit Desserts
66

Frozen Desserts, Ice Creams, *and* Sorbets
96

Foreword

by Jeremiah Tower

The history of classic desserts is usually considered to have begun with the great nineteenth-century French master Carême, who gave us recipes that were conceived in architectural terms, with plans as elaborate as those for intricate buildings. Later his disciple Urbain-Dubois, in his Le grand livre des pâtissiers et des confiseurs, simplified desserts, but even his designs—such as that for the famous Pêches à l'Andalouse—could easily have served as an elevation for the top of a turret of the Taj Mahal. Auguste Escoffier, heir to these teachers, went even further in streamlining desserts, to accommodate them to the changing tastes of the early twentieth century. Today, desserts have come to resemble, in any number of international settings, nothing so much as Schiaparelli hats, rarified concoctions whose creators seem to have only princely patrons, and imperial tastes, in mind.

Whether I am staying in superb hotels or dining in excellent restaurants, traveling in Hong Kong, Paris, London, Houston, New York, or Singapore, I have found that the dessert trolley has all but disappeared, the simple plate presentation has been banished to the cafés, and what is placed in front of the customer is once again a construction that looks like a reproduction in miniature of the truly fantastic astronomical temple of Jantar Mantar in India, a series of thin walls and cylindrical spiral staircases leading up to the heavens.

In the past seven years at Stars Restaurant, and more recently at Stars Café, we have avoided this trend toward flamboyance and instead sought to craft desserts that strike a sensible, alluring balance between appearance and taste. I believe that neither of these qualities should cancel the other out; rather, they should work together in harmony. The look of the dessert must create anticipation in a diner, and its taste a surprise that something complexly beautiful could be delicious; or, conversely, a visually simple dish like a blackberry crumble should be a revelation in the perfection of its flavor.

I do not mean to downplay the necessary element of humor, whimsy, and inspiration in the making of desserts, but a dessert that seeks equally to woo the diner's eye and then to flatter the taste buds is rarely, if ever, gratuitous. Sacha Guitry, in his preface to Edouard Nigon's playful book Eloges de la cuisine française (Paris, 1933), says: "Je ne deteste pas les choses inutiles, mais j'aime aussi beaucoup les choses necessaires." (I do not dislike things that are not useful, but I do like very much as well those *things that are necessary.) We have attempted at Stars, when studiously working on a new dessert, to have the final product look spontaneous. No dish should have the appearance or effect of painfully or torturously overworked deliberation, but should have instead a natural insouciance, an effortless elegance that is the result of an equilibrium of all its elements.*

The desserts of Stars' talented pastry chef, Emily Luchetti, who has headed the pastry kitchen for the past four years, are updated versions of American and European dishes, their concept and design always keeping in mind the original idea and, especially, the taste. They reflect truthfully their main ingredients, so that a chocolate dessert tastes like the finest chocolate, or a dessert using white peaches presents the diner with the full glory of a ripe, perfumed white peach, just touched with vanilla, sweet wine, and the briefest scent of raspberries. In Emily's desserts you will never see powdered sugar spread like a blizzard over the plate. You will not have to endure a mesh of caramel strands covering the dish like barbed wire over a field of battle. You will simply enjoy perfectly prepared desserts that do justice to the integrity of their components.

It is time again to take a stand for a cooking in which "simplicity of good taste" will be the guiding principle, while continuing to acknowledge that "simplicity does not necessarily rule out beauty," as Escoffier states in the introduction to Le guide culinaire, *a book dedicated to Urbain-Dubois, his master, as Escoffier is mine. In 1907 Escoffier intuited, helped define, and spectacularly fulfilled the culinary needs of the time. His is a powerful, modern, and always inspiring book in which he addresses those needs.* Le guide culinaire *is guided by two words of a now immortal phrase: "Faites simple." Emily Luchetti has honored that precept by allowing the freshest ingredients of the finest possible quality to be cooked and presented according to what they are, with only a minimum of enhancements, to create an appearance and a taste that are direct and true.*

Introduction

by Emily Luchetti

After working for several years in restaurant kitchens in New York, Paris, and San Francisco, I joined Stars when it opened in the summer of 1984. In less than a decade Stars has become an institution in San Francisco. An American rendition of the old brasseries of Europe and New York, it provides a gathering place with innovative food, fine service, and a lively atmosphere. Under its founder, Jeremiah Tower, Stars is also internationally recognized for being at the forefront of the culinary scene.

I spent several years cooking in the main part of Stars' kitchen and then switched to my longtime passion, desserts. While I appreciate the merits of other courses and feel that my experience with "savory" cooking has refined my palate and has given me the ability to create distinct desserts, preparing desserts has always given me a greater degree of satisfaction. Besides, at the end of the day, I would rather smell like chocolate and strawberries than garlic and shrimp!

As the pastry chef at Stars, I create a wide variety of desserts to match the diversity of our customers. A romantic couple at a corner table shares a warm chocolate pudding; an animated group in formal attire sips champagne and savors praline mocha napoleons; at the oyster bar, a casually dressed family enjoys maple pecan pie; businessmen and women conclude deals over espresso and cookie plates with Chinese almond drops and chocolate shortbread filled with mascarpone; in the private Grill Room, a tenth wedding anniversary party celebrates with peach-blueberry blintzes. Whatever the occasion or whomever the client, I am continually challenged to produce just the right dish.

An ideal dessert should be luscious, colorful, and composed, yet appear spontaneous and natural. In concept and design my own desserts are imaginative and interesting without being too technical or esoteric. Stars' desserts are updated versions of American and European classics without losing the essence of their original idea. They are familiar and inviting with an added flair and are straightforward in their composition. The ingredients I use are the freshest and of the best quality available. Chocolate desserts taste like rich bittersweet chocolate, peach desserts taste like ripe peaches. I do not mask the basic flavors of the ingredients. Components of each dessert stand on their own, but combined they enhance one another, and create something unforgettable. A flaky buttery crust becomes even better when filled with a tart lime mousse and mango; a chocolate almond torte is enriched when served with an orange custard sauce and espresso ice cream.

For Stars and Stars Café, the pastry cooks and I make seven different desserts daily, serving an average of 400 people a day. Each week we use 200 pounds of butter, 40 gallons of cream, 80 pounds of chocolate, 450 pounds each of sugar and flour, and over 1500 eggs. On a busy summer weekend we can easily use 10 cases of raspberries, 8 cases of boysenberries, 4 cases of strawberries, 2 cases of peaches, and a case of cherries.

The restaurant maintains a close relationship with its suppliers and depends on them to bring us the freshest and best produce, dairy products, and dry goods. I prefer to deal with several different chocolate companies, purchasing unsweetened chocolate from one, bittersweet and white chocolate from another, and extrabittersweet chocolate from yet a third. I use several different produce companies, each with its own areas of specialization. I feel that these relationships are vital to the success of my desserts, as fine ingredients are the starting points from which the best desserts are prepared.

The ovens are hot in Stars' pastry department long before most people in San Francisco have turned off their alarm clocks. My day begins with the production of pastries for Stars Café, including cinnamon rolls, oatmeal scones, and muffins. Next I review the menu from the night before, organize the production of the desserts we need to make that day, and discuss any last-minute changes with the pastry cooks. The maître'd has left us a note. It is a San Francisco socialite's birthday, and the hostess would like a heart-shaped cake with red hearts piped over it. We add the cake to the production list. I check to see if the daily produce order has come in and if it meets our standards for flavor and freshness. (The peaches are not ripe; they are sent back and replaced with some juicy, perfumed ones.) I verify the number of guests for the lunch and dinner parties in the private Grill Room. (The lunch party has increased by ten, and the chefs need puff pastry for hors d'oeuvres.) For the Stars kitchen, we make pizza dough and sheets of focaccia for the grilled vegetable sandwiches. This level of activity continues throughout the day as the pastry cooks scurry about melting chocolate, turning puff pastry, assembling trifles, frosting cakes, baking tarts and cookies, making sabayons, and freezing sorbets. The production is intense, and each cook executes several tasks at once. With the constant assistance of several timers (one being the cook's sense of when something is done), one learns to juggle all these different duties and stay one step ahead of them. We organize the desserts for lunch service, and I explain to the "commis" how to serve them. During the afternoon we continue making the evening's desserts and begin discussing the menu for the next day as we work.

When the evening pastry cooks arrive, I outline that night's work schedule. We review the presentation of all the desserts, including the best plates to use, and the appropriate sauces. New desserts are given to the waiters to taste. They ask about their ingredients and preparation so that they can describe them to their customers.

The evening service starts off quickly with many guests dining early before the symphony, ballet, or opera. Within an hour, the pastry cook has a long line of tickets in front of her. She rapidly plates cakes, sautés bananas for shortcakes, warms crêpes suzette, and at the same time keeps an eye out for the waiter whose desserts she's assembling. Like the production cook who works during the day, she performs many duties at once. Desserts are put together as fast as the tickets come in. Waiters are summoned for and not let out of the kitchen without several plates in both hands; hot desserts and soufflés must be served to the guests immediately and cannot be allowed to sit for even a moment. The evening continues and the pace remains furiously steady. Soon it is time for the after-dinner rush. We have a large number of guests who come to Stars just for desserts, stopping by to prolong an evening with a "nightcap" of a piece of mocha cream trifle or a tall glass filled with frozen Kir royale.

I vary the dessert menu daily, which allows us to take advantage of the best of seasonal produce. It is not unusual to switch the evening's desserts in the afternoon. A late arrival of delicious, sweet strawberries, ripened to perfection, should be immediately used in a tart with Grand Marnier cream. The fog in San Francisco can cause a quick change in the weather. A warm and soothing lemon pudding soufflé can ward off the chill and possibly even make one welcome the cold blast.

I am always thinking about new desserts and constantly trying different ideas and testing recipes. As I work throughout the day I exchange ideas with the pastry cooks. "What if we decreased the sugar in this recipe? Do you think the mousse would taste better if we used extrabittersweet chocolate instead of semisweet?" New desserts are created in various ways. Sometimes they are conceived as a group effort. One cook will envision an apple tart with a brown sugar custard and another will think of adding ground pecans to the tart *dough. Variations on desserts sometimes occur when two cooks work next to each other on separate projects. The sight of their ingredients placed side by side often suggests combinations that were not previously considered. One day a pastry cook was making fantasy cream, a rich mascarpone custard, while another was making a caramel sauce. I happened to walk by, saw the two at work, and caramel fantasy cream was born. To make certain a dessert has just the right flavor I test and taste, retest and taste again before putting it on the menu. Several attempts are often necessary before all the components come together to create a dessert that passes the inspection of Jeremiah and executive chef Mark Franz, and my own.*

I am often asked for dessert recipes. I have chosen and written the recipes in this book so that Stars desserts can be re-created in the home. The recipes are accessible to the home cook and most are not difficult to execute. Other recipes, although more involved, need only to be broken down into separate steps. As a result, this book is as useful to the dessert lover who is inexperienced in baking as it is to the more accomplished cook. Many people feel intimidated by baking because of its exacting properties. Baking depends on basic rules, but within these rules there is a great deal of flexibility. Baking is an enjoyable experience; it does not have to be an ordeal.

Preparing desserts can bring satisfaction on two levels. Presenting a beautiful raspberry-fig tart or a flavor-intense fruit trifle to friends or family brings creative fulfillment and the personal accomplishment of making a dessert. You also derive pleasure from seeing the dessert being enjoyed by others. As your creation is consumed and your guests smile and sigh with delight, you feel rewarded.

Although you may not have the same number of suppliers that are available to a professional pastry chef, there are places where you can get good-quality supplies. Investigate your local produce stores and inquire about the varieties of fruits available, when the freshest produce comes in, and what is grown locally. Local and mail-order cookware shops offer a wide selection of good-quality bakeware and baking ingredients.

In our desire to be healthy and physically fit, we do not have to sacrifice desserts. The key is moderation, not abstention. A maintained exercise program should be rewarded with an occasional bowl of hazelnut ice cream or a slice of apple-rhubarb pie. If we cannot eat desserts all the time, we must make sure that when we do, they are made of the best ingredients available and have the most intense flavor possible.

Custards, Puddings, *and* Trifles

1

*

The desserts in this chapter are often overlooked yet are

actually some of the best desserts around.

Custards are simple in design and small in size

but are fulfilling with their silky and creamy texture.

Steamed puddings do not have to be the cannonball variety

of winter holiday entertaining. Baked with steam, they are

just firm enough to be cut like a cake and are still very moist.

Trifles are ethereal, with complexity of flavors.

They are all based on the same principle: sponge cake layered

with various sauces and sabayons or flavored creams.

Trifles are wonderful for larger parties as they are dramatic,

and can be assembled a day ahead.

*

Caramel Pots *de* Crème

Caramel Custards are the epitome of all custards. Their intense
caramel flavor produces a rich, totally satiating dessert.
This is my favorite dessert. Serve with Russian Tea Cakes (page 198*).*
Serves 6

6 large egg yolks

1 cup sugar

¼ cup water

1 cup milk

2 cups heavy whipping cream

Six 6-ounce ovenproof ramekins

Preheat the oven to 300 degrees.

Place the egg yolks in a large mixing bowl and lightly whisk them. Set the bowl aside.

Dissolve the sugar in the water over low heat in a heavy-bottomed pot large enough to eventually hold the milk and cream. Increase to high heat and cook the sugar until it is a golden amber color. While the sugar is cooking, pour the milk and cream into a heavy-bottomed saucepot. Scald the mixture over medium high heat.

As soon as the caramel becomes a golden amber color, carefully and slowly pour the hot cream and milk into it. Use a long-handled spoon or whisk to mix them together, as the caramel will bubble as you begin to combine them.

Whisk the caramel cream into the egg yolks. Strain and refrigerate the custard base until cool. Skim any surface air bubbles off the custard base.

Pour the custard base into the ramekins. Place the ramekins in an ovenproof pan and put it in the oven. Fill the pan one-third to one-half full of hot water. (It is easier to fill the pan with water when it is already in the oven.) Cover the pan with aluminum foil.

Bake the pots de crème for about 50 minutes. When gently shaken, they should be set around the edges yet have an area in the middle, about the size of a quarter, that will not be completely firm.

Refrigerate the pots de crème for several hours to overnight.

Orange Crème Caramel *with* Raspberries

A crème caramel that is made even better
with the addition of orange and a few raspberries.
Serves 8

Custard Base:

6 large egg yolks

2 large eggs

1 cup sugar

Pinch salt

1 cup milk

3 cups heavy whipping cream

Peel of 2 oranges

Caramel:

1 cup sugar

⅓ cup plus 3 tablespoons water

1 pint raspberries

2 tablespoons Grand Marnier

Eight 6-ounce ovenproof ramekins

Preheat the oven to 300 degrees.

To make the custard base:
Put the egg yolks and eggs in a large stainless steel mixing bowl. Whisk in 1 cup sugar and salt. Set aside.

Pour the milk and cream into a heavy-bottomed saucepot. Add the orange peel and bring to a boil over high heat. Whisk the orange milk into the reserved egg yolk mixture.

Refrigerate the custard base until cool, and then strain it.

To make the caramel:
While the custard base is cooling, dissolve the remaining 1 cup sugar in the ⅓ cup water in a heavy-bottomed saucepot over low heat. Increase to high heat and cook the sugar until it is a golden amber color. Remove the pot from the heat and carefully and slowly stir in the 3 tablespoons water. Pour the caramel into the bottom of the ramekins. Set the ramekins aside to cool.

Pour the custard base into the caramel-lined ramekins. Place the ramekins in the ovenproof pan and put it in the oven. Fill the pan one-third to one-half full of hot water. (It is easier to fill the pan with water when it is already in the oven.) Cover the pan with aluminum foil. Bake the custards for about 50 minutes. The custards, when gently shaken, should be set around the edges yet have an area in the middle, about the size of a quarter, that will not be completely firm. Refrigerate several hours to overnight.

To serve, carefully run a small knife around the inside edge of each ramekin and unmold onto a plate. Toss the raspberries in the Grand Marnier. Scatter some raspberries around each custard.

Hazelnut Crème Caramel

A new flavor for a classic dessert. To skin hazelnuts
rub them in a clean towel while they are still warm from being toasted.

Serves 8

Custard:

6 large egg yolks

2 large eggs

1 cup sugar

Pinch salt

2¾ cups heavy whipping cream

1¼ cups milk

7 ounces hazelnuts, toasted,
    skinned, and coarsely chopped

Caramel:

1 cup sugar

⅓ cup plus 3 tablespoons water

Eight 6-ounce ovenproof ramekins

To make the custard base:
Preheat the oven to 300 degrees.

Put the egg yolks, eggs, sugar, and salt in a stainless steel bowl and whisk them together until smooth. Set aside.

Pour the cream and milk into a heavy-bottomed saucepot. Add the hazelnuts and scald the mixture. Turn off the heat, cover the pot, and let the hazelnuts steep in the milk for 15 minutes. Bring the hazelnut milk to a boil and slowly whisk it into the egg mixture. Cool the custard base to room temperature and strain.

To make the caramel:
While the custard base is cooling, place the sugar and ⅓ cup water in a heavy-bottomed saucepot. Over low heat, stir them together. When the sugar is dissolved, increase to high heat. Cook the sugar until it is a golden amber color. Remove the caramel from the heat and very carefully and slowly add the 3 tablespoons water. Pour the caramel into the bottoms of the ramekins. Set the ramekins aside to cool.

Pour the hazelnut custard base into the caramel-lined ramekins.

Put the ramekins in an ovenproof pan and put it in the oven. Fill the pan one-third to one-half full of hot water. (It is easier to fill the pan with water when it is already in the oven.) Cover the pan with aluminum foil and bake for about 50 minutes. When the custards are gently shaken, they will be set around the edges yet have an area in the middle, about the size of a quarter, that will not be completely firm.

Refrigerate the custards, several hours to overnight.

To serve, carefully run a small knife around the inside edge of each ramekin and unmold onto a plate.

Summer Trifle

I developed this recipe to create a trifle
that took advantage of many of summer's fruits.
Serves 8 to 10

4 large eggs, separated

⅓ cup sugar

Pinch salt

12 ounces mascarpone

½ teaspoon almond extract

2½ cups peaches (about 4), peeled
   and coarsely chopped

Pinch cream of tartar

¾ cup Blackberry Sauce (page 251)

¾ cup Raspberry Sauce (page 251)

1 recipe Sponge Cake (page 236)

A 2½-quart bowl

Put the yolks, sugar, and salt in the bowl of an electric mixer. With the whisk attachment, whip the mixture on high speed for about 3 minutes until it is thick. Add the mascarpone and almond extract and mix on medium speed until smooth and thick. Fold in the chopped peaches.

Put the egg whites in a separate bowl of an electric mixer. Using a clean, dry whisk attachment, whip them on medium speed until foamy. Increase to high speed, add the cream of tartar, and whip the whites until soft peaks form. Fold them into the almond cream.

To assemble the trifle:
Slice the sponge cake in half horizontally. Pour 2 tablespoons of the blackberry sauce in the bottom of the 2½-quart bowl and top with a ½-inch-thick layer of almond cream. Cut and fit cake pieces, forming a single layer over the cream. Soak the cake with about 2 tablespoons of the raspberry sauce and top with more almond cream.

Repeat this layering process, beginning again with the cake pieces, until the bowl is full, alternating the two berry sauces and ending with the almond cream.

Cover and refrigerate the trifle for at least 8 hours.

Spoon the trifle from the bowl and serve with remaining berry sauces.

Tropical Trifle
(see following page)

Tropical Trifle

This trifle was created for the opening of Jeremiah's Restaurant 690.
It will remind you of the tropics; all that is missing is a pink parasol!
The sabayon and sponge cake can be made a day in advance.
The flavor of trifles improves if they rest for 8 to 12 hours before serving.
Serves 8 to 10

6 large egg yolks

6 tablespoons sugar

Pinch salt

½ cup passionfruit liqueur

¾ cup heavy whipping cream

1 recipe Sponge Cake (page 236)

Double recipe Strawberry Sauce
   (page 251)

¼ cup dark rum

¾ cup pineapple juice

¾ cup sweetened coconut milk

1¼ cups blackberry jam, strained
   and thinned out with
   2 tablespoons water

A 2½-quart bowl

Fill a bowl one quarter full of ice water. Put the egg yolks, sugar, and salt in a large stainless steel bowl. Whisk until smooth. Add the passionfruit liqueur.

Put the bowl over a pot of boiling water and whisk the mixture vigorously until it is thick, tripled in volume, and mounds slightly when dropped from the whisk. This will take about 5 minutes.

Immediately put the bowl over the ice bath and whisk until cold.

Pour the cream into the bowl of an electric mixer and, using the whisk attachment, whip the cream on high speed until soft peaks form. Fold the cream into the cooked egg mixture. Refrigerate until ready to use.

To assemble the trifle:
Pour approximately ¼ cup of strawberry sauce into the 2½-quart bowl, covering the bottom.

Slice the sponge cake in half horizontally. Cut and fit cake pieces, forming a single layer over the strawberry sauce.

Sprinkle 2 teaspoons of the rum, 2 tablespoons of the pineapple juice, and 2 tablespoons of the coconut cream over the cake. Spread some of the blackberry jam and more of the strawberry sauce over the cake. Top with about ⅜ inch of passionfruit cream.

Repeat this layering process beginning again with cake pieces, until the bowl is full, ending with the passion fruit cream.

Cover and refrigerate the trifle for at least 8 hours before serving with the following mango sauce.

Mango Sauce

*

3 medium-sized ripe mangoes
2 tablespoons sugar
Small pinch salt

*

To make the mango sauce:
Peel the mangoes and remove the pulp
from the pit.

*

Put the mango pulp in a food processor fitted
with the metal blade and purée it. Strain the
purée through a medium-holed strainer, pour it
into a small bowl, and mix in the sugar and salt.
Refrigerate until ready to use.

Lemon Blueberry Trifle

A beautiful summer trifle, made even better
when it is served with custard sauce.
Serves 8 to 10

6 cups blueberries

6 tablespoons Simple Syrup
  (page 250)

1 teaspoon freshly squeezed
  lemon juice

1¾ cups heavy whipping cream

2 tablespoons sugar

1½ cups Lemon Curd (page 237)

1 recipe Sponge Cake (page 236)

A 2½-quart bowl

Put the blueberries, simple syrup, and lemon juice in a heavy-bottomed saucepot. Cook over medium heat until the berries begin to give off some of their liquid.

Purée half of the blueberries in a food processor fitted with the metal blade. Stir the purée back into the other blueberries. Reserve 1 cup of blueberry sauce for later use.

Put the cream and sugar in the bowl of an electric mixer. With the whisk attachment, whip on high speed until soft peaks form. Fold the whipped cream into the lemon curd.

To assemble the trifle:
Slice the sponge cake in half horizontally. Spread a thin layer of blueberry sauce in the bottom of the bowl and top with ½ inch of lemon cream. Cut and fit cake pieces, forming a single layer over the lemon cream.

Repeat the layering process until the bowl is full, ending with the lemon cream.

Cover the trifle and refrigerate for at least 8 hours.

To serve, spoon the trifle from the bowl and top with the reserved blueberry sauce.

Mocha Cream Trifle

Chocolate cake and espresso cream combined with
Cognac make this an elegant yet easily assembled dessert.
Serves 8

<u>Espresso cream:</u>

6 large egg yolks

1 cup sugar

1 cup espresso

1 cup milk

2½ tablespoons cornstarch

1½ ounces bittersweet chocolate,
  finely chopped

1 teaspoon vanilla extract

1½ cups heavy whipping cream

<u>Cognac Syrup:</u>

¾ cup Simple Syrup (page 250)

1 tablespoon Cognac

1 recipe Chocolate Sponge Cake
  (page 236)

1 recipe Cognac Custard Sauce
  (page 246)

A 2½-quart bowl

To make the espresso cream:
Place the egg yolks and sugar in a medium-sized bowl. Whisk until thick. Stir in the espresso, the milk, and then the cornstarch.

Transfer the espresso milk to a noncorrosive heavy-bottomed saucepot. Stirring constantly with a rubber spatula, cook the mixture over medium low heat for about 10 minutes, until thick. Be sure to scrape the bottom of the pot or the espresso milk will stick and burn. Remove the pot from the stove and stir in the chocolate and vanilla extract.

Strain the espresso mixture through a strainer. Transfer it to a stainless steel bowl. Place plastic wrap directly on the surface to prevent a skin from forming. Refrigerate the espresso base until cool.

Put the heavy cream in the bowl of an electric mixer. Using the whisk attachment, whip on high speed until soft peaks form. Fold it into the espresso cream. Refrigerate the cream until you are ready to assemble the trifle.

For the Cognac syrup:
Stir together the simple syrup and the Cognac. Set aside.

To assemble the trifle:
Slice the sponge cake in half horizontally. Pour a ¼- to ½-inch-thick layer of espresso cream in the bottom of the 2½-quart bowl. Cut and fit cake pieces, forming a single layer over the espresso cream. Brush the cake with some of the Cognac syrup and again top with espresso cream.

Repeat the layering process, beginning with cake pieces, until the bowl is full, ending with the espresso cream.

Cover and refrigerate for at least 8 hours.

Spoon the trifle from the bowl and serve with cognac custard sauce.

Tiramisù

I first had tiramisù in a small restaurant in Lucca, Italy.
I did not know what it was, but it looked fabulous on the pastry cart,
served in a large ceramic bowl. Many variations use ladyfingers
and add liqueur, but we prefer this one made with sponge cake and espresso.
Serves 8 to 10

6 large eggs, separated

½ cup sugar

Pinch salt

1 pound mascarpone

Pinch cream of tartar

1 recipe Sponge Cake (page 236)

2½ cups chocolate shavings

1¾ cups cold espresso or very
   strong, rich coffee

A 2½-quart bowl

Put the egg yolks, sugar, and salt in the bowl of an electric mixer. Using the whisk attachment, whip on high speed for about 3 minutes, until thick. Add the mascarpone and mix on medium speed until smooth and thick.

Put the egg whites in a separate bowl of an electric mixer. Using a clean, dry whisk attachment, whip them on medium speed until foamy. Increase to high speed, add the cream of tartar, and whip until soft peaks form. Fold the egg whites into the mascarpone cream.

To assemble the tiramisù:
Slice the sponge cake in half horizontally. Pour a ⅜-inch-thick layer of the mascarpone cream in the bottom of the 2½-quart bowl and sprinkle chocolate shavings on top. Cut and fit cake pieces, forming a single layer over the mascarpone cream. Brush the cake with some of the espresso and top with more mascarpone cream and chocolate shavings.

Repeat this layering process, beginning again with the cake pieces, until the bowl is full, ending with the chocolate shavings.

Cover and refrigerate the trifle for at least 8 hours before serving.

To serve, spoon from the bowl.

Lemon Custards

If you are at loss for a quick, simple, and delicious lunch or dinner dessert,
this is the one. Serve with Ginger Cookies (page 190).
Serves 8

6 large egg yolks

2 large eggs

1 cup sugar

¾ cup plus 1 tablespoon freshly
   squeezed lemon juice

2½ cups heavy whipping cream

Eight 6-ounce ovenproof ramekins

Preheat the oven to 300 degrees.

Put the egg yolks, eggs, and sugar in a stainless steel bowl and whisk them until smooth. Stir in the lemon juice and the cream. Strain the lemon custard base and skim off any air bubbles.

Pour the custard into the ramekins. Put the ramekins in an ovenproof pan and put it in the oven. Fill the pan one-third to one-half full of hot water. (It is easier to fill the pan with water when it is already in the oven.) Cover the pan with aluminum foil and bake the custards for about 50 minutes. The custards, when gently shaken, will be set around the edges yet have an area in the middle, about the size of a quarter, that will not be completely firm.

Refrigerate the custards, several hours to overnight.

Before serving, let the custards sit at room temperature for 15 minutes.

Ginger Crème Brûlée

The trick to producing a good brûlée is simply to have a rich,
ultrasmooth custard and then to melt the sugar on top of it
into an ice-rink-hard, paper-thin caramel without melting the custard.
If you do not have a crème brûlée iron or a very hot broiler,
put the custards in a pan of ice water to keep them firm
while you broil the sugar.
Serves 8

6 large eggs yolks

2 large eggs

¾ cup granulated sugar

Pinch salt

1½ cups milk

2¾ cups heavy whipping cream

1 ounce fresh ginger root, roughly
   chopped

6½ tablespoons superfine sugar

Eight 6-ounce ovenproof ramekins

Preheat the oven to 300 degrees.

Put the egg yolks, eggs, granulated sugar, and salt in a stainless steel bowl. Whisk the mixture together.

Pour the milk and the cream into a heavy-bottomed saucepot. Add the ginger and scald the mixture. Slowly whisk it into the egg mixture. Cool the custard base and strain it through a medium-holed strainer.

Pour the custard into the 8 ramekins. Skim off any air bubbles.

Put the ramekins in an ovenproof pan and put it in the oven. Fill the pan one-third to one-half full of hot water. (It is easier to fill the pan with water when it is already in the oven.) Cover the pan with aluminum foil and bake the custards for about 50 minutes. When the custards are gently shaken, they will be set around the edges yet have an area in the middle, about the size of a quarter, that will not be completely firm.

Refrigerate the custards several hours to overnight.

To serve:
Preheat the broiler until it is very hot. Sprinkle the 6½ tablespoons superfine sugar over the ginger custards. Place the custards approximately 3 inches from the broiler. Broil until the sugar is caramelized. Allow the sugar to harden for a couple of minutes and then serve.

Mango Strawberry Fool

Dessert "fools" are fresh fruit purées folded into softly whipped cream.
Their silly name belies a delicious summertime dessert.
Serves 6

8 ripe medium-sized mangoes

1½ cups heavy cream

Pinch salt

2 tablespoons sugar

3 pints strawberries, hulled and
   thinly sliced

2 tablespoons dark rum

Peel the mangoes and remove the flesh from the pits. Purée the mango flesh in a food processor fitted with the stainless steel blade. Pass the purée through a medium-sized strainer. Set aside.

Put the cream, salt, and sugar in a stainless steel mixing bowl and whisk until soft peaks form. Fold the cream and the mango purée together. Refrigerate until ready to serve.

To serve:
Put the strawberries in a bowl and toss them with the dark rum. Put the strawberries in individual dessert glasses and top with the mango cream.

Blancmange

*Superb eating, and definitely worth the slight effort required,
this sublime bavarian cream is perhaps the best dessert to eat with Sauternes,
with or without raspberries. This is an adaptation of a Richard Olney recipe.
It must be started the day before you plan to serve it.*

Serves 6

4 ounces whole natural (skin on)
   almonds

¼ teaspoon bitter almond essence

6 tablespoons water

1 cup milk

1 tablespoon almond oil or
   unflavored oil

1½ teaspoons gelatin

2 tablespoons water

½ cup sugar

6 tablespoons heavy whipping
   cream

Six 3-ounce stainless steel molds or
   one 1-quart stainless steel mold

Blanch the almonds for 15 seconds in boiling water. Drain them and peel off their skins.

Put the almonds and 6 tablespoons water in a food processor fitted with the metal blade. Finely grind them to make a paste. Transfer the almond paste to a bowl and mix in the 1 cup milk. Cover the almond milk and refrigerate overnight.

The following day, brush a 1-quart metal mold or six 3-ounce metal molds with the oil and invert to drain out any excess. Set aside.

Strain the almond milk through a strainer lined with cheesecloth. Fold the cheesecloth around the ground nuts and twist the ends in opposite directions, extracting as much milk as possible. There should be a little over ¾ cup of almond milk. Stir the sugar into the almond milk and set aside.

Place the gelatin in a small pot and pour the 2 tablespoons water over it. Let the gelatin sit for 5 to 10 minutes. Dissolve the gelatin over low heat. Remove it from the heat and stir the gelatin into the almond milk.

Place the bowl of almond milk over an ice bath until it begins to set. Whip 6 tablespoons of cream until soft peaks form. Fold the whipped cream into the almond mixture. Add the almond essence.

Pour the almond cream into the prepared mold(s) and refrigerate until set, 4 to 6 hours.

To unmold, dip the mold(s) into hot water for 5 seconds and invert onto a plate or plates. Serve the blancmange plain or with raspberries.

Pear Cornmeal Bread Pudding

The grated nutmeg over the top of this pudding is a nod
to its Indian pudding heritage and is also mysteriously wonderful with pears.
These puddings can be reheated in a 325-degree oven for 10 minutes.
Serves 8

7 large eggs

5 large egg yolks

1 cup sugar

Pinch salt

2½ cups heavy whipping cream

3½ cups milk

One-inch piece vanilla bean

1½ pounds pears, peeled, cored,
   and diced into ½-inch pieces

5 slices Cornmeal Poundcake (page
   163), cut into pieces 1 inch by
   ½ inch

½ teaspoon freshly grated nutmeg

1 recipe Chantilly Cream
   (page 252)

One 2½-quart baking dish
   3 inches deep

Whisk together the eggs, egg yolks, sugar, and salt in a stainless steel bowl. Set the mixture aside.

Put the cream, milk, and vanilla bean in a heavy-bottomed saucepot and scald. Slowly whisk the hot milk mixture into the egg mixture. Cool and strain the custard base.

Preheat the oven to 325 degrees.

Place the pears in the bottom of the baking dish. Arrange the cake pieces on top of the pears. Pour the custard base over the pears. Grate ¼ teaspoon of the nutmeg on top.

Bake the pudding, uncovered, for 55 to 60 minutes. A paring knife inserted into the custard should come out almost completely clean.

To serve the pudding, spoon some into bowls. Top with the chantilly cream and the remaining ¼ teaspoon of grated nutmeg.

Walnut Rum Steamed Pudding

This steamed pudding is suitable in both winter and summer.
In the summer serve it with brandied peaches, Peach Ice Cream (page 117),
and Blackberry Sauce (page 251). In the winter serve it with coffee custard and caramel sauces.
Serves 8 to 10

5 ounces walnuts, toasted and
   finely chopped

1½ cups sugar

6 ounces (1½ sticks) soft sweet
   butter

4 large eggs

3 tablespoons dark rum

1½ cups flour

Pinch salt

¾ teaspoon baking soda

1½ teaspoons baking powder

A 2-quart steamed pudding mold

Butter the underside of the top and the inside of a 2-quart steamed pudding mold.

Sprinkle 2 tablespoons of the chopped walnuts in the bottom of the mold.

Put the sugar and the butter in the bowl of an electric mixer. With the paddle attachment, cream on medium speed, just until smooth. Continuing to mix, add the eggs two at a time. Stir in the rum and the remaining walnuts.

Sift together the flour, salt, baking soda, and baking powder. On low speed, fold the dry ingredients into the batter. Spread the batter into the mold and cover the mold with the lid.

Put the pudding in a pot large enough to enclose the mold with at least a 2-inch clearance all around the mold. Fill the pot with hot water one-third of the way up the sides of the mold. Cover the pot and bring the water to a simmer.

Check the water periodically during the cooking process to make sure that the water is just simmering. (Rapidly boiling water will cause the pudding to rise prematurely and then sink.) Steam the pudding for about 1½ to 2 hours. A skewer inserted in the middle should come out clean.

Cool the pudding completely before unmolding and slicing.

Pumpkin Steamed Pudding

A fall alternative to pumpkin pie.
Serves 8 to 10

6 ounces (1½ sticks) soft sweet
   butter

2¼ cups sugar

3 large eggs

3 tablespoons freshly squeezed
   lemon juice

1½ cups Pumpkin Purée
   (page 241)

2¼ cups flour

½ teaspoon ground ginger

2¼ teaspoons baking powder

¾ teaspoon salt

1¼ teaspoons ground cinnamon

¼ teaspoon ground allspice

1 recipe Chantilly Cream
   (page 252)

½ cup warm Caramel Sauce
   (page 238)

A 2-quart steamed pudding mold

Butter the underside of the top and the inside of the pudding mold.

Put the butter and the sugar in the bowl of an electric mixer. With the paddle attachment, cream on medium speed until light and fluffy.

Continuing to mix, beat in the eggs one at a time. Add the lemon juice and the pumpkin purée.

Sift together the flour, ground ginger, baking powder, salt, cinnamon, and allspice. On low speed, stir the dry ingredients into the pumpkin mixture.

Spread the batter into the mold and cover the mold with the lid. Place the pudding in a pot large enough to enclose the mold with at least a 2-inch clearance all around the mold. Fill the pot with hot water one-third of the way up the sides of the mold. Cover the pot and bring the water to a low simmer.

Check the water periodically during the cooking process to make sure the water is just simmering. (Rapidly boiling water will cause the pudding to rise prematurely and then sink.) Steam the pudding for about 1½ to 2 hours. A skewer inserted in the middle should come out clean.

Cool the pudding completely before unmolding.

Serve the pudding with chantilly cream and warm caramel sauce.

Blueberry Steamed Pudding

*Steamed puddings do not have to be the traditional, heavy variety associated with
English country houses (which are made with suet); they can be very light without losing
the "comfort food" quality of a pudding. This one, a recipe from my great-grandmother Florence,
shows that even after fifty years, its simplicity and clear flavors make it a natural addition
to the Stars' menu and to anyone's menu.*

Serves 8 to 10

1½ cups blueberries

½ cup sugar

1 teaspoon lemon juice

¼ teaspoon plus a pinch salt

1½ cups flour

½ teaspoon baking soda

1 teaspoon baking powder

¾ teaspoon ground ginger

1 teaspoon chopped lemon zest

½ cup molasses

½ cup milk

1 large egg

1 tablespoon sweet butter, melted

1 recipe Chantilly Cream

   (page 252)

1 recipe Blueberry Sauce (page 251)

A 2-quart steamed pudding mold

Butter the underside of the top and the inside of a 2-quart steamed pudding mold.

Put the blueberries in a bowl. Toss them with the sugar, lemon juice, and the pinch of salt. Place them in the bottom of the steamed pudding mold.

Sift together the flour, baking soda, baking powder, ginger, and the ¼ teaspoon salt. Stir in the lemon zest. Set aside.

In a large bowl, whisk together the molasses, milk, egg, and melted butter. Add the dry ingredients to the molasses mixture and mix until smooth. Pour the batter into the mold over the blueberries and cover the mold with the lid.

Put the mold in a pot large enough to enclose the mold with at least a 2-inch clearance all around the mold. Fill the pot with hot water one-third of the way up the sides of the mold. Cover the pot and bring the water to a simmer.

Check the water periodically during the cooking process to make sure that the water is just simmering. (Rapidly boiling water will cause the pudding to rise prematurely and then sink.) Steam the pudding for about 1 hour. A skewer inserted in the middle should come out clean.

Let the pudding cool for 10 minutes and then invert it onto a plate.

Slice the pudding while it is still warm and serve with chantilly cream and blueberry sauce.

Persimmon Pudding

A real fall dessert. Serve this with Chantilly Cream (page 252)
and a sprinkle of cinnamon. To ripen persimmons, put them
in the freezer overnight, and thaw them; they will be ready to use.
Serves 8

3 large eggs

1 cup sugar

4 ounces (1 stick) sweet butter,
   melted

1½ cups flour

1 teaspoon baking soda

1 teaspoon baking powder

½ teaspoon ground ginger

½ teaspoon ground cinnamon

½ teaspoon ground allspice

Pinch ground cloves

½ teaspoon salt

2 cups half and half

2 cups persimmon purée, strained
   (2 or 3 whole persimmons)

A 9-inch square pan

Preheat the oven to 350 degrees.

Butter the pan.

Put the eggs and sugar in the bowl of an electric mixer. Using the paddle attachment, beat them on medium speed until well combined. Add the melted butter.

Sift together the flour, baking soda, baking powder, ginger, cinnamon, allspice, cloves, and salt. Stir these dry ingredients into the egg mixture. Slowly pour in the half and half. Add the persimmon purée. (Be sure to add the purée last, as the mixture will get very thick if you do not.)

Pour the batter into the prepared pan and bake the pudding for about 40 minutes, until a skewer inserted in the middle comes out clean. The pudding will sink as it cools.

Serve the pudding warm. It can be reheated for 15 minutes in a 325-degree oven.

Chocolate Pudding

*A chocolate pudding just as good as mom used to make.
It tastes even better if you make a hole in the middle just before
serving and pour in some heavy cream.*

Serves 6

6 large egg yolks

2 tablespoons plus 1 teaspoon sugar

Pinch salt

2 teaspoons vanilla extract

2½ cups heavy whipping cream

3½ ounces bittersweet chocolate,
   finely chopped

Six 6-ounce ovenproof ramekins

Preheat the oven to 300 degrees.

Whisk together the egg yolks, sugar, salt, and vanilla in a large bowl. Set aside.

Scald 1 cup of the cream in a heavy-bottomed saucepot and then add the chocolate. Cover and let stand for 5 minutes. Stir until the mixture is smooth and no chocolate pieces remain.

In a separate saucepot, scald the remaining 1½ cups cream and whisk it into the chocolate cream. Slowly pour the chocolate cream into the egg yolk mixture and whisk until smooth.

Pour the pudding base into the ramekins. Place them in an ovenproof pan and put it in the oven. Fill the pan one-third to one-half full of hot water. (It is easier to fill the pan with water when it is already in the oven.) Cover the pan with aluminum foil and bake the puddings for about 40 minutes. The puddings, when gently shaken, should be set around the edges yet have an area in the middle, about the size of a half dollar, that will not be completely firm. Be careful not to overcook them. As they cool, they will set more.

Refrigerate the puddings several hours to overnight, but let them sit at room temperature for 15 minutes before serving.

If desired, serve with additional heavy cream.

Summer Pudding

This dessert signifies summer to me more than any other.
You can use a mixture of mixed berries, and red currants are a nice addition.
Serves 8

3 pints strawberries, stemmed and

    quartered

½ cup sugar

2 pints blackberries

2 pints raspberries

1 teaspoon freshly squeezed

    lemon juice

2 tablespoons framboise liqueur

Pinch salt

32 pieces Brioche (page 244), sliced

    ³⁄₁₆ inch thick, crusts removed

1 recipe Chantilly Cream

    (page 252)

Eight 6-ounce ramekins, each

    3 inches wide and 3 inches deep

Put the strawberries and sugar in a saucepot and cook over medium low heat for approximately 10 minutes, until the strawberries begin to give up some of their juice. Add the blackberries and raspberries and continue cooking until the berries have broken apart, about 10 minutes more. Cool the berry mixture and add the lemon juice, framboise, and salt to taste.

Cut the brioche into 3-inch circles.

Pour about 1½ tablespoons of the berry "sauce" into the bottom of each ramekin. Dip a piece of the brioche into the sauce, saturating the bread. Place the berry-soaked brioche in the ramekin. Spoon a tablespoon of berry sauce on top of the bread. Continue layering the puddings in this manner until the ramekins are very full, almost overflowing.

Cover the puddings with wax paper or plastic wrap. Place them on a baking sheet and cover with another pan or large pot and a 3 to 5 pound weight, compressing the puddings. Refrigerate overnight.

Unmold the puddings by running a paring knife along the inside edge of each ramekin and inverting them.

Serve with chantilly cream.

Hot Desserts

2

*

Hot desserts should not be limited to rainy nights
and elegant dinner parties. Stars' hot desserts are striking
in appearance and effect but are not difficult to make.
Compotes can primarily be prepared ahead and quickly assembled
at the last minute. Contrary to popular belief, it is not
necessary to tiptoe past the oven and speak in hushed tones
while a soufflé is baking. Soufflés, like big dogs,
just need to be treated with a little respect. Egg whites are delicate,
should not be overwhipped, and should be folded
gently into the soufflé base.

*

Chocolate Hazelnut Crêpes

*The richness of chocolate and mascarpone combined with
the crunchy filling and warm sauce makes this a perfect winter dessert.*
Serves 6

2 ounces hazelnuts, toasted,
    skinned, and coarsely chopped

8 ounces mascarpone

¼ cup plus 1 teaspoon hazelnut
    liqueur, such as Frangelico

1 tablespoon sugar

2 tablespoons heavy whipping cream

1 cup Simple Syrup (page 250)

3 tablespoons orange juice

1 teaspoon freshly squeezed
    lemon juice

Pinch salt

2 ounces (½ stick) sweet butter

12 Chocolate Crêpes (page 243)

½ cup warm Chocolate Sauce
    (page 237)

A 12-inch sauté pan

Combine the hazelnuts, the mascarpone, 1 teaspoon of the Frangelico, the sugar, and the cream in a small bowl. Mix until combined. Set aside.

Fold the crêpes into quarters.

Heat the ¼ cup Frangelico, simple syrup, the orange juice, the lemon juice, and the salt in a large sauté pan over medium heat. Place half of the crêpes in the pan and cook them for 15 to 30 seconds, until they are warmed through. Remove them from the pan and keep them warm on a covered plate while you cook the remaining crêpes. Remove the second batch of crêpes from the pan and place them with the first batch. Add the butter to the pan and continue to cook the sauce until it begins to thicken.

Place two crêpes on each plate. Spoon some sauce over the crêpes and top with the hazelnut mascarpone cream.

Drizzle the warm chocolate sauce over the crêpes. Serve immediately.

Crêpes Suzette

*Escoffier originally made crêpes suzette with tangerine juice
and Curaçao and we believe it is still the purest and best version,
so at Stars we do the same.*

Serves 6

1¼ cups freshly squeezed
    tangerine juice

1½ teaspoons freshly squeezed
    lemon juice

3 tablespoons orange Curaçao

3 tablespoons Simple Syrup
    (page 250)

12 crêpes (page 242)

3 ounces (¾ stick) sweet butter

A 12-inch sauté pan

Heat the tangerine and lemon juices, Curaçao, and simple syrup in a large sauté pan over medium-high heat. Put half the crêpes in the pan and cook for 15 to 30 seconds, until they are warmed through. Remove them from the pan, and keep them warm on a covered plate while you cook the remaining crêpes. Remove the second batch from the pan and place them with the first batch.

Add the butter to the pan and continue to cook the sauce until it begins to thicken.

Put two crêpes, folded into quarters, on each plate. Spoon some warm sauce over the crêpes and serve immediately.

Raspberry Pistachio Crêpes

What better excuse to have a dessert wine than as an accompaniment to
pistachios and raspberries—both born for Sémillon or even Sauvignon sweet wines.
Use chopped strawberries, if you wish, in place of the raspberries.

Serves 6

4 ounces toasted unsalted pistachios

1 tablespoon sugar

6 tablespoons Simple Syrup

    (page 250)

1 teaspoon chopped orange zest

12 Crêpes (page 242)

¼ cup light rum

1¼ cups freshly squeezed

    orange juice

1 teaspoon freshly squeezed

    lemon juice

Pinch salt

2 ounces (½ stick) sweet butter

2 cups raspberries

A 12-inch sauté pan

Place the pistachios and sugar in a food processor fitted with the metal blade. Grind them finely. Transfer the ground pistachios to a small bowl and mix them with 3 tablespoons of the simple syrup and the orange zest to form a paste.

Put about 2 teaspoons of the pistachio paste on each crêpe, 1 inch from the edge. Roll the crêpes up, tucking the ends in as you go. "Glue" the end of each crêpe to its underside with a little of the pistachio paste. Set aside.

Heat the rum, orange juice, lemon juice, the remaining 3 tablespoons of simple syrup, and salt in a large sauté pan over medium-high heat. Place the crêpes, seam side down, in the pan. Cook them for 1 minute, gently turn them over, and cook them for another 30 seconds. They should just be warmed through.

Carefully put 2 crêpes on each plate. Return the pan to the burner and increase the heat to high. Add the butter and cook the sauce until it begins to thicken. Remove the pan from the heat, gently mix in the raspberries, and pour the sauce over the crêpes.

Serve immediately.

Nectarine Blueberry Blintzes

*Blintzes are small, thin, crêpelike cakes filled with
savory or sweet fillings. Here they are combined
with rich mascarpone and topped with warm fruit.*

Serves 6

12 ounces mascarpone

1 tablespoon sugar

¾ teaspoon vanilla extract

Pinches salt

12 Crêpes (page 242)

3 tablespoons clarified sweet butter

4 cups peeled and sliced nectarines
  (about 6)

2 cups blueberries

½ cup Simple Syrup
  (page 250)

2 tablespoons lemon juice

2 ounces (½ stick) sweet butter

A 12-inch sauté pan

In a small bowl, mix together the mascarpone, sugar, vanilla extract, and a small pinch of salt.

Put about 2 teaspoons of the mascarpone mixture on each crêpe, 1 inch in from the edge. Roll the crêpe up, tucking the ends in as you go. "Glue" the end of the crêpe to its underside with a little of the mascarpone. (The blintzes can be assembled ahead and refrigerated, if desired.)

In a large sauté pan, heat the clarified butter. Add the blintzes, seam side down, and cook for a minute or two, until browned. Carefully turn them over and brown the other side. The blintzes should be warm in the middle. Be careful that the mascarpone cream does not leak out. Remove the blintzes from the pan, set them aside, and keep them warm while you make the sauce.

Put the nectarines, blueberries, simple syrup, lemon juice, and a pinch of salt in the pan. Cook the fruit for several minutes over medium high heat until it is warmed through. Place 2 blintzes on a plate. With a slotted spoon, spoon the fruit over the blintzes. Add the butter to the pan, bring to a boil, and cook until the sauce begins to thicken. Divide the sauce evenly over the blintzes and serve immediately.

Lemon Raspberry Pudding Soufflé

This is a wonderful dessert, half light soufflé, half creamy pudding.
It can sit for 5 to 10 minutes if you are not quite ready for it.
This is also delicious using passionfruit juice in place of the lemon juice.
Serves 6 to 8

1½ cups raspberries

3 ounces (¾ stick) sweet soft butter

1 cup sugar

4 large eggs, separated

½ cup freshly squeezed and
    strained lemon juice

½ cup flour

¼ teaspoon salt

2¼ cups milk

⅛ teaspoon almond extract

2 tablespoons Simple Syrup
    (page 250)

Powdered sugar for dusting

A 2-quart ovenproof soufflé dish

Place the raspberries in the bottom of the soufflé dish.

Put the butter and sugar in the bowl of an electric mixer. Using the paddle attachment, cream them on medium high speed for 2 minutes, until light. Beat in the egg yolks, one at a time. On medium low speed, add the lemon juice, flour, and salt, and then the milk. (This part of the batter can be made ahead. Refrigerate it until you are ready to bake the soufflés.)

Preheat the oven to 325 degrees.

Choose a roasting pan large enough to hold the soufflé dish, and put it in the oven. Fill it one-quarter full of water.

Put the egg whites in a clean bowl of an electric mixer. With the whisk attachment, whip them on medium speed until frothy. Increase to high speed and continue whipping until soft peaks form. Fold the egg whites into the lemon mixture.

Pour the batter over the raspberries in the soufflé dish.

Put the soufflé dish in the prepared pan. The water should come at least one-third up the sides of the dish. Add or remove water as necessary.

Bake the pudding soufflé, uncovered, for 60 to 65 minutes, until the top is golden brown and the sides are pulling away from the sides of the dish.

Remove it from the oven. Mix together the almond extract and the simple syrup in a small bowl and brush mixture over the top of the pudding soufflé.

Dust with powdered sugar and serve warm.

Pear Soufflé *with* Ollalieberry Sauce

Another fruit soufflé, this one is immeasurably improved
(unless you have your own ancient variety of pear trees) by a tablespoon of
Poire William or pear eau de vie for its perfume.
Serves 8

5 ripe pears, peeled and sliced
   ½ inch thick

7 tablespoons sugar

1 tablespoon pear liqueur

1½ teaspoons freshly squeezed
   lemon juice

Pinch salt

¾ cup egg whites (about 6)

½ teaspoon cream of tartar

Powdered sugar for dusting

1 recipe Ollalieberry Sauce
   (page 251)

A 1½-quart ovenproof soufflé dish

Put the pear slices in a 12-inch sauté pan. Add 6 tablespoons of the sugar, the pear liqueur, lemon juice, and salt. Cook the pears over medium heat until they are soft.

Put the pear mixture in a food processor fitted with the metal blade and purée. Pour the purée into a heavy-bottomed saucepot. Cook, stirring often, for about 10 to 15 minutes, until thick. Refrigerate the purée until it is cold.

Preheat the oven to 350 degrees.

Butter and sugar the soufflé dish.

Put the egg whites in the bowl of an electric mixer. Using the whisk attachment, whip them on medium speed until frothy. Increase to high speed, add the cream of tartar, and whip until soft peaks form. Continue whipping and slowly add the remaining 1 tablespoon sugar in a steady stream. Whip until the egg whites are stiff but not dry.

Fold the pear purée into the egg whites. Do not completely incorporate; the soufflé batter should still have slight streaks of pear purée. Carefully spread the batter in the prepared dish. Tap the dish gently on the counter and swirl the top with your finger, making a slight peak in the middle of the soufflé.

Bake the soufflé for about 20 to 25 minutes, until it is set and slightly browned. The middle will still be creamy.

Dust the top of the soufflé with the powdered sugar and serve it immediately with the ollalieberry sauce on the side.

Praline Soufflé *with* Chocolate Custard Sauce

Caramel and chocolate are two flavors that are made for each other.
Both have strong tastes, so one does not overpower the other.
Serves 8

Soufflé Base:

3 large egg yolks

⅓ cup sugar

½ cup flour

Pinch salt

1½ cups milk

3-inch piece vanilla bean

To assemble and bake the soufflé:

1 tablespoon butter

2 tablespoons sugar

¾ cup egg whites (about 6)

½ teaspoon cream of tartar

Pinch salt

¾ cup ground Praline (page 250)

A 2-quart ovenproof soufflé dish

Powdered sugar for dusting

Chocolate Custard Sauce

   (page 246)

To make the soufflé base:
Whisk together the egg yolks and sugar in a stainless steel bowl. Stir the flour and the salt into the egg mixture.

Bring to a boil a pot of water that is large enough to hold the stainless steel bowl so that it sits halfway down in the pot.

Scald the milk with the vanilla bean in a heavy-bottomed saucepot. Whisk the milk into the egg mixture.

Put the bowl over the pot of simmering water and cook the soufflé base, whisking constantly, for a couple of minutes, until the mixture thickens. Whisk until smooth. Remove from the stove and cover the base with plastic wrap directly on the surface to prevent a skin from forming. Refrigerate until cold.

Preheat the oven to 350 degrees.

Butter and sugar the inside of the soufflé dish with the 1 tablespoon of butter and the 2 tablespoons of sugar.

Put the egg whites in the bowl of an electric mixer. With the whisk attachment, whip them on medium speed until foamy. Add the cream of tartar and salt. Increase to high speed and continue whipping until stiff but not dry. Stir the praline into the vanilla base. Fold in the whites.

Carefully spread the batter in the prepared dish and gently tap the dish on the counter. Bake the soufflé for about 30 to 35 minutes, until golden brown and firm around the edges.

Dust the soufflé with powdered sugar and immediately serve with chocolate custard sauce.

Plum Soufflé *with* Orange Custard Sauce

To bring out the intense flavors of fruit purées for these soufflés,
we substituted all egg whites for the usual egg yolk base. They create a dramatic
look as they rise beautifully. The most ethereal soufflé Jeremiah ever baked
was made from wild strawberries for James Beard in 1976.

Serves 6

1 pound ripe plums (about 9),
  pitted and cut into eighths

½ cup plus 1 tablespoon sugar

1 teaspoon freshly squeezed
  lemon juice

Pinch salt

Powdered sugar for dusting

¾ cup egg whites (about 6)

½ teaspoon cream of tartar

1 recipe Orange Custard Sauce
  (page 246)

A 1½-quart ovenproof soufflé dish

Put the plum slices in a large sauté pan. Add ½ cup of the sugar, the lemon juice, and salt. Cook the mixture over medium heat until the plums are soft.

Put the plum mixture in a food processor fitted with the metal blade and purée. Strain through a medium-holed sieve to eliminate the skins. There should be about 1½ cups of purée. Refrigerate the purée until it is cold.

Preheat the oven to 350 degrees.

Butter and sugar the inside of the soufflé dish.

Put the egg whites in the bowl of an electric mixer. Using the whisk attachment, whip them on medium speed until frothy. Increase to high speed, add the cream of tartar, and whip until soft peaks form.

Continue whipping and slowly add the remaining 1 tablespoon of granulated sugar in a steady stream. Whip until the egg whites are stiff but not dry.

Fold the plum purée into the egg whites. Do not completely incorporate; the soufflé batter should still have slight streaks of plum purée. Gently spread the batter in the prepared dish. Tap the dish gently on the counter and swirl the top with your finger, making a slight peak in the middle of the soufflé.

Bake the soufflé for 20 to 25 minutes, until golden brown. The middle will still be creamy.

Dust the top of the soufflé with the powdered sugar and serve immediately with the orange custard sauce on the side.

Poppyseed Orange Soufflé

For an even more dramatic entrance, soufflés can be made in individual servings.
Bake them in 12-ounce porcelain ramekins.
Serves 8

Soufflé Base :

1½ cups milk

1 teaspoon chopped lemon zest

¼ cup poppyseeds

3 large egg yolks

⅓ cup sugar

½ cup flour

Pinch salt

To assemble and bake the soufflé:

1 tablespoon butter

2 tablespoons sugar

¾ cup egg whites (about 6)

½ teaspoon cream of tartar

Pinch salt

A 2-quart ovenproof soufflé dish

Powdered sugar for dusting

1 recipe Framboise Custard Sauce

(page 246)

To make the soufflé base:
Scald the milk with the lemon zest and poppyseeds in a heavy-bottomed saucepot. Turn off the heat, cover the pot, and steep the milk for 10 minutes.

Whisk together the egg yolks and sugar in a stainless steel bowl. Stir the flour and salt into the egg mixture. Whisk the poppyseed milk into the egg mixture.

Bring to a boil a pot of water that is large enough to hold the stainless steel bowl so that it sits halfway down in the pot.

Put the bowl over the pot of simmering water and cook the soufflé base, whisking constantly, for a couple of minutes, until the mixture thickens. Whisk until smooth. Remove from the stove and cover the base with plastic wrap directly on the surface to prevent a skin from forming. Refrigerate until cold.
Preheat the oven to 350 degrees.

Butter and sugar the inside of the soufflé dish with the 1 tablespoon of butter and the 2 tablespoons of sugar.

Put the egg whites in the bowl of an electric mixer. With the whisk attachment, whip them on medium speed until foamy. Add the cream of tartar and salt. Increase to high speed and continue whipping until stiff but not dry. Fold the whites into the poppy-seed base.

Carefully spread the batter in the prepared dish and gently tap the dish on the counter. Bake the soufflé for about 30 to 35 minutes, until golden brown and firm around the edges. (The center of the soufflé will still be creamy.)

Dust the soufflé with powdered sugar and immediately serve it with framboise custard sauce on the side.

Cappuccino Soufflé

*Stars is known for its "made to order" soufflés. Hollyce Snyder,
the pastry sous-chef, has been crowned Queen of Soufflés.
She once simultaneously served eighteen individual soufflés to one table!*

Serves 8

Soufflé Base:

1½ cups milk

⅔ cup crushed espresso beans

3 large egg yolks

⅓ cup sugar

½ cup flour

Pinch salt

1 recipe Cinnamon Custard Sauce
   (page 246)

To assemble and bake the soufflé:

1 tablespoon butter

2 tablespoons sugar

¾ cup egg whites (about 6)

½ teaspoon cream of tartar

Pinch salt

A 2-quart ovenproof soufflé dish

Powdered sugar for dusting

To make the soufflé base:
Scald the milk and the espresso beans in a heavy-bottomed saucepot. Turn off the heat, cover the pot, and steep the espresso beans in the milk for 10 minutes.

Put the egg yolks in a stainless steel bowl and whisk in the sugar. Stir in the flour and salt.

Bring to a boil a pot of water that is large enough to hold the stainless steel bowl so that it sits halfway down in the pot.

Strain the beans from the milk through a fine strainer. Whisk the espresso-flavored milk into the egg yolk mixture.

Put the bowl over the pot of simmering water and cook the soufflé base, whisking constantly, for a couple of minutes, until the mixture thickens. Whisk until smooth. Remove it from the stove and cover the base with plastic wrap directly on the surface to prevent a skin from forming. Refrigerate until cold.

Preheat the oven to 350 degrees.

Butter and sugar the inside of the soufflé dish with the 1 tablespoon butter and the 2 tablespoons sugar.

Put the egg whites in the bowl of an electric mixer. With the whisk attachment, whip them on medium speed until foamy. Add the cream of tartar and salt. Increase to high speed and continue whipping until stiff. Fold the whites into the cappuccino base.

Gently spread the batter in the prepared dish and gently tap the dish on the counter. Bake the soufflé for about 30 to 35 minutes, until golden brown and firm around the edges. (The center of the soufflé will still be creamy.)

Dust the soufflé with powdered sugar and serve immediately, with cinnamon custard sauce on the side.

Bittersweet Chocolate Pudding

This pudding is actually made up of two parts: a thick, rich pudding over a chocolate sauce. It is a simple and very comforting dessert and is best served with heavy cream.

Serves 6

6 ounces (1½ sticks) soft sweet butter

1½ cups firmly packed brown sugar

3 large eggs

1 teaspoon vanilla extract

1⅓ cups all-purpose flour

¼ teaspoon salt

¾ teaspoon baking soda

⅓ cup plus 1½ teaspoons cocoa
   powder

2 tablespoons water

6 tablespoons hot water

3 tablespoons powdered sugar

1½ cups heavy whipping cream

A 2-quart ovenproof dish

Preheat the oven to 350 degrees. Place in the oven a roasting pan large enough to hold the ovenproof dish. Fill it one-quarter full of water.

Place the butter and 1 cup of the brown sugar in the bowl of an electric mixer. Using the paddle attachment cream on medium high speed for 2 minutes, until light. Continue to mix, slowly add the eggs and then the vanilla extract.

Sift together the flour, salt, baking soda, and the ⅓ cup of cocoa powder. Increase to low speed and stir the dry ingredients into the creamed mixture. Stir in the 2 tablespoons of water. Spread the batter in the ovenproof dish.

In a small bowl, mix together the remaining ½ cup brown sugar, 1½ teaspoons cocoa powder, and the 6 tablespoons hot water. Pour the cocoa liquid over the top of the chocolate batter.

Put the pudding in the water bath in the oven. The water should come halfway up the sides of the baking dish. Add or take out water as necessary.

Bake the pudding for 55 to 60 minutes. When done, the top of the pudding will be cracked and will have pulled away from the sides of the dish. A skewer inserted in the middle of the pudding should come out clean.

Remove the pudding from the oven and sprinkle the top with the 3 tablespoons of powdered sugar. Serve warm with the heavy cream on the side.

Maple Banana Compote
with Ginger Ice Cream

This is American comfort food at its best.
The cool and spicy flavors of the ginger ice cream mingle
with the warm maple syrup and bananas to create
a very soothing and delicious combination.
Serves 6

3 tablespoons firmly packed
　brown sugar

1⅓ cups freshly squeezed
　orange juice

⅓ cup pure maple syrup

1 teaspoon freshly squeezed
　lemon juice

⅓ cup dark rum

Pinch salt

3 ounces sweet butter

4 cups bananas, peeled and sliced
　¼ inch thick on a slight diagonal
　(5 medium-sized bananas)

6 scoops Ginger Ice Cream
　(page 120)

1 ounce pecans, toasted and coarsely
　chopped

Whisk together the brown sugar, orange juice, and maple syrup in a mixing bowl. Stir in the lemon juice, rum, and salt.

Pour the mixture into a large sauté pan and bring it to a boil over medium heat. Add the butter and reduce the sauce until it thickens slightly and reduces by about half. This will take several minutes. Add the bananas and continue to cook the sauce for 2 or 3 minutes, until the bananas are warmed through.

Put a scoop of ice cream into each bowl and spoon some of the bananas and the sauce on top. Sprinkle with the pecans.
Serve immediately.

Strawberry Compote
with Rhubarb Ice Cream

A new delicious twist to an old and favorite combination.

Serves 8

2 tablespoons freshly squeezed
   lemon juice

5 tablespoons sugar

5 tablespoons Grand Marnier

4¾ cups strawberries, hulled and
   thinly sliced

2 ounces (½ stick) sweet butter

8 Orange Shortbread cookies
   (page 203)

8 scoops Rhubarb Ice Cream
   (page 118)

Combine the lemon juice, sugar, and Grand Marnier in a 12-inch sauté pan. Bring the liquid to a boil over medium high heat. Add strawberries and then the butter. Continue cooking, stirring gently, for 2 minutes, just until the butter is melted.

Put an orange shortbread and a scoop of the rhubarb ice cream on each plate. Top with the strawberry compote. Serve immediately.

Black Mission Fig Raspberry Gratin

Figs and raspberries belong together. Here is a Russian-inspired
marriage of flavors that is simple and devastatingly delicious.
Serves 6

8 large egg yolks

½ cup sugar

Pinch salt

½ cup freshly squeezed orange juice

¼ cup amaretto, preferably
    Amaretto di Saronno

1 cup heavy whipping cream

12 black mission figs, cut into
    eighths (about 3½ cups)

1½ cups raspberries

2 tablespoons framboise

Powdered sugar

A 2½-quart ovenproof dish 2 to
    3 inches deep

Fill a bowl one quarter full of ice water and set aside. Whisk together the egg yolks, sugar, and salt in a stainless steel bowl until smooth. Add the orange juice and amaretto. Place the bowl over a pot of boiling water and whisk the mixture vigorously for about 5 minutes, until it is thick and tripled in volume. It will mound slightly when dropped from a whisk. Immediately put the bowl over the ice bath and whisk the sabayon until it is cold.

Put the cream in the bowl of an electric mixer. Using the whisk attachment, whip on high speed until soft peaks form. Fold the whipped cream into the cooled sabayon. Refrigerate the sabayon until ready to use.

Preheat the broiler, and preheat the oven to 400 degrees. In a bowl combine the figs, raspberries, and framboise. Place the fruit mixture in the shallow ovenproof dish. Put the dish in the oven for 8 minutes, remove, and immediately spoon the amaretto sabayon over the fruit. Broil the gratin until golden brown, about 3 minutes. Dust with powdered sugar. Serve immediately.

Fruit Desserts

3

*

The entrance of summertime and its fruits and berries

is long anticipated at Stars. After working all winter using citrus,

persimmons, nuts, and chocolate, I am excited to have

the fresh tastes and vibrant colors of summer fruits.

Bing cherries, so juicy and dark in color that they stain your fingers

as you pit them; succulent peaches with blushed pink skins;

baskets of fragrant and plump ollalieberries and raspberries;

lusciously red and sugar-ripe strawberries;

deep purple skinned plums with red-pink interiors;

these fruits are all signs that summer has arrived.

*

Riesling Poached Peaches

A beautiful, simple, and elegant dessert
that becomes sublime if you use white peaches.
Serves 6

6 medium-sized peaches, ripe but
    still slightly firm

2 cups gewürztraminer

1 cup late harvest Riesling

2 cups Simple Syrup (page 250)

1 tablespoon freshly squeezed
    lemon juice

1¾ cups water

¾ cup freshly squeezed orange juice

Pinch salt

2 pieces lemon peel, about ¼ inch
    wide and 2 inches long

4 pieces orange peel, about ¼ inch
    wide and 2 inches long

1 recipe Chantilly Cream
    (page 252)

1 recipe Raspberry Sauce
    (page 251)

Halve and pit the peaches. Reserve the pits.

Combine the gewürztraminer, Riesling, simple syrup, lemon juice, water, orange juice, salt, and lemon and orange peels in a large nonaluminum saucepot. Bring the liquid to a boil.

Reduce the heat to a simmer and add the peaches. Cover them with a clean dish towel or plate to completely submerge them in the liquid. Cook at a simmer for 15 to 20 minutes just until the peaches can be pierced easily with a small knife. Transfer them to a metal bowl and place them over an ice bath.

Cool and then peel the peaches. Save the peelings.

Add the reserved pits and the skins to the poaching liquid and bring it back to a boil. Reduce it to 1¼ cups; it should be slightly syrupy. Cool and then strain the syrup.

To serve, spoon some of the syrup on the bottom of each plate, place two peach halves on the plate, and top with chantilly cream and raspberry sauce.

Poached Pears *with* Walnut Cream

The secret to poaching pears is slow, careful cooking and
a good-quality Sauternes like Château Liot or a California equivalent.
Serves 6

The pears:

6 ripe but firm pears, peeled and
   halved

2½ cups good quality Sauternes

1 cup Simple Syrup (page 250)

½ cup water

One ½-inch piece orange peel

One ½-inch piece lemon peel

One 2-inch piece cinnamon stick

Pinch salt

2 tablespoons freshly squeezed
   lemon juice

Walnut Cream:

2 ounces toasted walnuts

2 ounces mascarpone

1 teaspoon chopped orange zest

1 tablespoon sugar

Pinch salt

½ teaspoon hazelnut liqueur,
   such as Frangelico

¾ cup heavy whipping cream

To make the pears:
Carefully scoop out the cores of the pears with a melon baller or a small spoon.

Put the Sauternes, simple syrup, water, orange and lemon peel, cinnamon stick, salt, and lemon juice in a medium-sized non-aluminum pot. Bring the liquid to a boil.

Reduce the heat so that the liquid is simmering and add the pear halves. Cover the pears with a clean dish towel or plate to completely submerge them in the liquid. Simmer for about 20 minutes, just until the pears can be pierced easily with a small knife.

Transfer the pears to a bowl and cool them over an ice bath. Return the liquid to the stove and reduce it over medium-high heat until it begins to get slightly syrupy. This will take 5 to 10 minutes. Cool and then strain the syrup. (The sauce will get thicker as it cools.)

To make the walnut cream:
Put the walnuts in a food processor fitted with a metal blade and finely grind them. Combine all of the other ingredients in the bowl of an electric mixer. With the whisk attachment, whip the cream mixture until it begins to thicken but has not yet reached soft peaks. Add all but ¼ cup of the walnuts and continue whipping until soft peaks form. Refrigerate until ready to use.

To assemble:
Arrange 2 pear halves, flat side up, on each plate and fill each with 1 tablespoon of the walnut cream. Drizzle the pear syrup over and around the pears and sprinkle with the remaining ground walnuts.

Savarin *with* Grand Marnier Sabayon *and* Mixed Berries

*Named for Brillat-Savarin, this classic dessert is
seldom made nowadays, but its versatility will never go out of style.
During winter serve the savarins warm with warm apples and cider sabayon.*

Serves 8

Savarin dough:

1½ teaspoons dry yeast

2 tablespoons water

1½ teaspoons sugar

2 tablespoons warm milk

2 large eggs

1 cup flour

2½ ounces soft sweet butter

¼ teaspoon salt

*8 savarin molds, 3 inches in diameter
and ½ inch deep, or one 11-inch
ring mold*

To make the savarin:

Mix the yeast and the water in the bowl of an electric mixer using the paddle attachment on low speed. Stir in the sugar and let stand for 10 minutes. Add the warmed milk and then the eggs, mixing on low speed until incorporated. Add the flour and beat just until smooth.

Transfer the dough to a stainless steel bowl, cover, and let rise for 2 to 4 hours, until doubled.

Place the dough in an electric mixer. Using the paddle attachment, add the soft butter and salt. Mix until the butter is completely incorporated. Transfer the dough to a stainless steel bowl and let it rise until doubled. (As this point the dough may be refrigerated and allowed to rise overnight.)

Butter the savarin molds or ring mold. Press the dough into the mold(s). The dough will be sticky, and is easier to work with if you coat your fingertips with butter. Cover the mold(s) with a pan or bowl, giving them enough clearance so that they can double in volume. Let rise for 1 to 2 hours, until doubled.

Preheat the oven to 350 degrees.

Bake the savarin(s) for 15 to 20 minutes, until light brown.

2 cups Simple Syrup (page 250)
2 tablespoons freshly squeezed lemon juice
¼ cup Grand Marnier
¼ cup freshly squeezed orange juice

6 cups raspberries, blackberries, blueberries
in combination
1 recipe Grand Marnier Sabayon (page 245)
2 cups Raspberry or Blackberry Sauce (page 251)

*

To serve:
Mix together the simple syrup, lemon juice,
Grand Marnier, and orange juice in a shallow pan.
Place the savarin(s) in the syrup and soak them in the
syrup for 15 minutes on each side.

Serve the savarins with the berries, Grand Marnier
sabayon, and berry sauce.

Vanilla Wafer Cookies *with* Zinfandel-marinated Raspberries

Red wine and red fruit have been traditionally matched
(Cabernet sauce and strawberries, with black pepper, for example),
and here the peppery quality of the zinfandel goes very well with raspberries.
Use the presentation with various cooked or marinated fruits.

Serves 8

Vanilla Wafer Cookies:

2 egg whites

½ cup plus 1 tablespoon sugar

3 ounces (¾ stick) butter, melted

½ teaspoon vanilla extract

½ cup plus 1 tablespoon flour

Zinfandel-marinated Raspberries :

1½ cups fruity zinfandel

7 tablespoons sugar

Three ¼-inch strips orange rind

Two ¼-inch strips lemon rind

Small pinch ground cinnamon

¾ cup water

4 peppercorns

6 cups raspberries

To serve:

Chantilly Cream (page 252)

Preheat the oven to 350 degrees.

To make the vanilla wafers:
Whisk the egg whites and sugar together in a stainless steel bowl just until incorporated. Whisk in the melted butter, vanilla extract, and then the flour.

Line a baking sheet with parchment paper.

For each cookie, spread out approximately 1 tablespoon of the batter in a thin even circle about 4 inches in diameter, using the back of a tablespoon. You should be able to fit 6 circles on a sheet pan.

You will have more batter than you will need for 16 wafers. Make a few extra wafers, as they are fragile and can break easily.

Bake the wafers for about 5 minutes until golden brown. Check often, as they burn quickly.

When cool, remove the cookies from the pan with a thin flat metal spatula. Wrap them airtight until ready to use.

To make the raspberries:
Combine the zinfandel, sugar, orange and lemon rinds, cinnamon, water, and peppercorns in a small saucepot over high heat. Bring the liquid to a boil, lower heat, and simmer for 20 minutes. Remove the liquid from the heat, cool, and strain it.

Pour the sauce over the raspberries. Let them marinate for 30 minutes.

To serve:
Put a cookie on each plate, top with raspberries, a few tablespoons of the zinfandel liquid, some chantilly cream, and another wafer.

Plum Crisp *with* Cornmeal Cinnamon Streusel

The addition of cornmeal in the streusel topping gives
this crisp added crunch, color, and flavor. Serve with Chantilly Cream (page 252).
Serves 6

6 cups ½-inch slices of ripe plums

   (about 12 plums)

3 tablespoons sugar

1 teaspoon freshly squeezed

   lemon juice

Pinch salt

Streusel:

½ cup light brown sugar

1 teaspoon ground cinnamon

½ cup flour

½ cup yellow cornmeal

4 ounces (1 stick) sweet cold butter

A 2-quart ovenproof dish

Preheat the oven to 350 degrees.

Combine the sliced plums with the sugar, lemon juice, and salt in a large bowl. Put the mixture in the ovenproof dish.

To make the streusel:
Put all the streusel ingredients in a food processor. With pulsing turns, mix until the butter is pea-sized. Sprinkle the streusel over the plums. Bake the crisp for about 30 minutes, until the fruit is bubbly and the streusel is lightly browned.

Serve the crisp warm.

Strawberry Rhubarb Crisp

Tapioca flour is used here because it thickens quickly and doesn't leave a floury taste.
Serve the crisp warm with vanilla ice cream.

Serves 8

3½ cups ¼-inch-thick slices
    rhubarb

4 cups strawberries, hulled and
    sliced

½ cup sugar

2 tablespoons tapioca flour

1 tablespoon freshly squeezed
    lemon juice

Pinch salt

The streusel:

½ cup light brown sugar,
    firmly packed

4 ounces (1 stick) cold sweet butter

¼ teaspoon salt

1 cup flour

2 teaspoons chopped orange zest

A 1½-quart ovenproof dish

Preheat the oven to 350 degrees.

Put the rhubarb and the strawberries in a large bowl. Combine the sugar, tapioca flour, lemon juice, and salt in a small bowl. Mix the sugar mixture with the fruit and place the fruit in the ovenproof dish. Set it aside while you make the streusel.

To make the streusel:
Put all the streusel ingredients in a food processor fitted with the metal blade. Using pulsing turns, process until the butter is pea-sized. Sprinkle the streusel over the strawberry rhubarb mixture.

Bake the crisp for 30 to 35 minutes, until the fruit is bubbly and the streusel is lightly browned. Serve warm with vanilla ice cream.

Apple Pandowdy

For this and all apple desserts, use firm and juicy apples. Every region of the country has its own varieties, so search out the best in your area. Serve the pandowdy warm with Caramel Ice Cream (page 116) and warm Caramel Sauce (page 238).

Serves 8

7 medium-sized apples, peeled,
    cored, and sliced ⅛ inch thick

4 ounces (1 stick) sweet butter

½ cup sugar

2 tablespoons freshly squeezed
    lemon juice

1 teaspoon ground cinnamon

½ teaspoon ground allspice

¼ teaspoon ground ginger

Pinch ground cloves

Pinch salt

1 cup heavy whipping cream

1 cup golden raisins

The topping:

1½ cups flour

4 ounces pecans, toasted and
    finely chopped

Pinch salt

3 tablespoons sugar

2 teaspoons baking powder

3 ounces (¾ stick) sweet butter

¾ cup heavy whipping cream

A 1½-quart ovenproof dish.

Preheat the oven to 350 degrees.

Put the apple slices, butter, sugar, lemon juice, cinnamon, allspice, ginger, cloves, and salt in a large pot. Cook over medium heat until the apples are soft but still retain their shape.

Add the cream to the pan and continue to cook the apples for about 5 minutes, until the liquid has thickened slightly. Depending on how juicy the apples are, this can take from 5 to 15 minutes.

Stir in the golden raisins. Place the apple mixture in the ovenproof dish and set it aside while you make the pecan topping.

To make the topping:
Combine the flour, pecans, salt, sugar, and baking powder in the bowl of an electric mixer. Using the paddle attachment on low speed, mix the butter into the dry ingredients until it is the size of small peas. Continue to mix and add the cream, mixing just until the dough comes together.

On a lightly floured board roll the dough ¼ inch thick. Cut it into eight 3-inch circles. Place the circles on top of the apple mixture.

Bake the pandowdy for 30 to 35 minutes, until the topping is golden brown and the apples are beginning to bubble around the edges. Serve warm in bowls with caramel ice cream and caramel sauce.

Pear Charlotte

We use brioche when making charlottes because it produces a crispier, richer crust.
The charlottes can be made ahead and reheated.
Serves 8

7 ripe pears, peeled, cored, and
    sliced ¼ inch thick

⅔ cup plus 1 tablespoon sugar

Pinch salt

1 tablespoon pear liqueur

1½ tablespoons freshly squeezed
    lemon juice

1 loaf Brioche (page 244) sliced
    3/16 inch thick, crusts removed

4 ounces (1 stick) sweet butter

1 teaspoon ground cinnamon

1 recipe Vanilla Custard Sauce
    (page 246)

1 recipe Chantilly Cream
    (page 252)

Eight 6-ounce ramekins 3 inches in
    diameter and 1½ inches deep

Preheat the oven to 350 degrees.

Put the pear slices in a large sauté pan with ⅔ cup sugar, the salt, pear liqueur, and lemon juice. Cook the mixture, stirring occasionally, over medium heat for about 10 minutes, until the pears are soft. Set aside to cool.

Place the butter, the remaining 1 tablespoon of sugar, and the cinnamon in the bowl of an electric mixer. Using the paddle attachment on medium speed, cream the mixture until it is smooth.

Butter each piece of brioche with the cinnamon butter. With the long side of the bread closest to you, cut each slice into 3 pieces. Line the sides of the ramekins with the brioche pieces, butter side against the ramekin.

Compactly fill the inside of each ramekin with about ¼ cup of the pear mixture. Trim off any brioche that sticks up above the ramekin.

Bake the charlottes for 15 to 20 minutes, until the brioche is toasted. Unmold and serve warm with vanilla custard sauce and chantilly cream.

Peach Boysenberry Cobbler

Like crisps, cobblers need no ingredients other than fruit and a rich, buttery topping,
because the taste of the fresh ripe fruit is the point of these desserts.

Serves 8

5 cups ¼-inch slices of peeled,
   pitted peaches (about 6 large)

2 tablespoons tapioca flour

5 tablespoons sugar

1 teaspoon freshly squeezed
   lemon juice

Pinch salt

1½ cups boysenberries

Cobbler Topping:

2 cups flour

½ teaspoon salt

¼ cup firmly packed light
   brown sugar

2 teaspoons baking powder

3 ounces (¾ stick) sweet cold butter

¾ cup plus 2 tablespoons heavy
   whipping cream

1 recipe Chantilly Cream
   (page 252)

A 2-quart ovenproof dish

Preheat the oven to 350 degrees.

Combine the peaches with the tapioca
flour, sugar, lemon juice, and salt in a large
bowl. Gently mix in the boysenberries.
Place the mixture in the ovenproof dish.
Set aside.

To make the topping:
Combine the flour, salt, 3 tablespoons of the
brown sugar, and baking powder in the bowl
of an electric mixer. Using the paddle attachment add the butter on low speed and mix
until it is the size of large peas. Continue to
mix and slowly add ¾ cup of the cream.
Mix just until combined. On a lightly floured
board, roll the dough ½ inch thick. Using a
3-inch star cutter, cut the dough into star
shapes. Place them on top of the peach mixture. Brush the tops with the remaining
2 tablespoons of cream. Sprinkle the remaining 1 tablespoon of brown sugar on top.

Bake the cobbler for 25 to 30 minutes, until
the topping is golden brown.

Serve the cobbler warm with chantilly cream.

Hollyce's Sin Pot

This naturally fermented fruit compote is unusual in its preparation and appearance.
It may look unappealing as it ages, but when you taste it with ice cream you will ask for
seconds. As a cool refreshing drink, combine the strained liquid with seltzer water
and serve over ice. Use caution, however, as it packs a wallop.
Makes about 4 cups

Starter:

11 cups roughly sliced fresh fruit
(see Note)

11 cups sugar

Mix 4 cups of the fruit and 4 cups of the sugar together in a large bowl. Transfer the fruit to a clean gallon size glass jar, cover the jar with a double layer of cheesecloth, and wrap a rubber band around the rim. Gently stir the fruit every day for 2 weeks.

Every other day during this 2-week period, add and stir in an additional 1 cup of fruit and an additional 1 cup of sugar. After the 2 weeks, let the sin pot sit for 1 month in a cool place and stir it every few days. It will give off a lot of juice as it sits and will begin to ferment.

To serve:
Spoon the sin pot over vanilla ice cream with your choice of cookies.

The sin pot will keep for several months at room temperature.

Note:
Use only cherries, peeled peaches, nectarines, or plums in the first 2 weeks. Later on you can add pears, apples, strawberries, blackberries, or raspberries. Do not use citrus fruits or blueberries.

French Sweet Cream *with* Raspberries *and* Blackberries

Julia Orenstein, a pastry cook at Stars, created this dessert, which has the creamy consistency of custard but is rich in flavor, like a cheesecake.

Serves 6

2 teaspoons gelatin

2 tablespoons cold water

1 cup heavy whipping cream

½ cup sugar

14 ounces sour cream

3 ounces mascarpone

1½ teaspoons vanilla extract

1 tablespoon freshly squeezed
   lemon juice

2 cups raspberries

2 cups blackberries

1½ cups Berry Sauce (page 251)

Six 6-ounce ramekins

In a small bowl, sprinkle the gelatin over the cold water and let it stand for 10 minutes.

Whisk together the heavy cream, sugar, sour cream, and mascarpone in a large stainless steel mixing bowl. Place the bowl over a pot of simmering water.

When the cream mixture is warm, dissolve the gelatin over low heat and whisk it into the cream. Continue heating the mixture, stirring occasionally, until it is hot, about 150 degrees. Stir in the vanilla extract and lemon juice. Strain the custard through a fine strainer.

Pour the custard into the ramekins. Refrigerate the French creams for several hours until set.

To serve:
Unmold each cream by dipping the ramekins in hot water for several seconds. Run a knife around the inside edge of the ramekin and invert the cream onto a plate. Serve with the raspberries, blackberries, and berry sauce.

Plum Tartlets *with* Vanilla Pastry Cream

Use straight-sided tart shells for these. You can make
shallow ½-inch tartlets or "deep dish" tartlets, in which case use more pastry cream.
The vanilla in the cream works perfectly with the flavor of the plums.
Serves 6

10 ripe plums, thin-skinned
variety, cut into sixths
3 tablespoons sugar
Pinch salt
½ teaspoon freshly squeezed
lemon juice
Six 4-inch prebaked tart shells
(see page 240)
2 cups vanilla Pastry Cream
(page 239)

Put the plums in a large sauté pan with the sugar, salt, and lemon juice. Cook them over medium heat for 5 to 10 minutes, until they are soft and give off some juice but still retain their shape. As the plums cook, stir them gently so as not to break them up.

To assemble:
Spoon some pastry cream into the tart shells, top with the warm plums, and serve immediately.

Caramel Fantasy Cream *with* Peaches

A favorite of Jeremiah's, this dessert has an ethereal quality.
The only way to describe its texture and flavor is "luscious."
It is best served the day it is made.
Serves 6 to 8

6 large egg yolks

¼ cup sugar

Pinch salt

1 pound mascarpone

½ cup cold Caramel Sauce
   (page 238)

3 large egg whites

Pinch cream of tartar

6 ripe medium-sized peaches,
   peeled and sliced

Put the egg yolks, sugar, and salt in the bowl of an electric mixer. On high speed, with the whisk attachment, whip the mixture until it is thick and pale yellow. Add the mascarpone and caramel sauce and again whip until thick.

Put the egg whites in a separate bowl of an electric mixer. With a clean whisk attachment, whip on medium low speed until frothy. Add the cream of tartar, increase to high speed, and continue to whip until soft peaks form. Fold the egg whites into the mascarpone cream. Refrigerate the caramel fantasy cream until ready to use.

To serve:
Put the peach slices in bowls or large long-stemmed wine glasses and spoon the cream over the peaches.

Poppyseed Shortcakes *with* Strawberries

*At Stars we have reworked this traditional American dessert
in a variety of ways, but what counts in any version is a hot buttered
shortcake laden with berries, cream, and berry sauces.*

Serves 6

2½ cups flour

¼ cup plus 2 tablespoons sugar

2½ tablespoons poppyseeds

3¼ teaspoons baking powder

½ teaspoon salt

4 ounces (1 stick) cold sweet butter

1 cup plus 3 tablespoons heavy
   whipping cream

2 tablespoons soft sweet butter

3 cups strawberries, hulled and
   sliced

3 cups Chantilly Cream (page 252)

1 cup Berry Sauce (page 251)

Preheat the oven to 350 degrees.

Combine the flour, ¼ cup of sugar, poppy-seeds, baking powder, and salt in the bowl of an electric mixer. Using the paddle attachment on low speed, add the cold butter and mix until it is the size of small peas. Continue to mix and slowly add 1 cup plus 2 tablespoons of the cream. Mix just until the dough comes together.

On a lightly floured board, roll the dough 1 inch thick and cut it into six 3-inch circles. Brush the remaining 1 tablespoon of cream on top of the shortcakes and then sprinkle on the remaining 2 tablespoons of sugar.

Bake the shortcakes for 20 to 25 minutes, until golden brown.

To assemble:
Split the shortcakes in half and butter them with the 2 tablespoons of soft butter. Warm them in the oven. Place some strawberries, cream, and berry sauce over the bottom half of each shortcake. Top with the second half of the shortcake and dollop with more cream and berry sauce.

Almond Shortcakes *with* Raspberries *and* Lemon Cream

Another version of our popular shortcakes, also to be served warm.
It is important to use the lemon curd on the day it is made.

Serves 6

3 ounces toasted sliced almonds

1½ cups flour

½ teaspoon salt

½ cup sugar

2½ teaspoons baking powder

3 ounces (¾ stick) cold sweet butter

2½ cups plus 2 tablespoons heavy
    whipping cream

1 recipe Lemon Curd (page 237)

2 tablespoons soft sweet butter

3 cups raspberries

2 cups Berry Sauce (page 251)

Preheat the oven to 350 degrees.

Put the almonds in a food processor fitted with the metal blade and finely grind them.

Combine the ground almonds, flour, salt, 3 tablespoons of the sugar, and the baking powder in the bowl of an electric mixer.

Using the paddle attachment on low speed, add the cold butter and mix until the butter is the size of small peas. Continue to mix, and slowly add ½ cup of the cream, just until the dough comes together.

On a lightly floured board, roll the dough 1 inch thick and cut it into six 3-inch circles. Brush 2 tablespoons of cream on top of the shortcakes and then sprinkle on 2 tablespoons of sugar.

Bake the shortcakes for 25 to 30 minutes, until golden brown.

To make the lemon cream:
Put the remaining 2 cups of cream and 3 tablespoons of sugar in the bowl of an electric mixer. Using the whisk attachment, whip the cream to soft peaks. Fold in the lemon curd. Refrigerate the lemon cream until ready to serve the shortcakes.

To assemble:
Split the shortcakes in half and butter them with the 2 tablespoons of soft butter. Warm them in the oven. Put some lemon cream on the bottom half of each shortcake, and top with raspberries, a little more lemon cream, some berry sauce, and then the top half of the shortcake.

Blackberry Napoleons
with Tangerine Sabayon

*Summer's fresh, juicy, plump blackberries are perfectly highlighted here
by flaky, buttery puff pastry and a subtle tangerine sabayon.
If you can find ollalieberries or boysenberries, both varieties of
blackberries, use them, as they are generally sweeter and juicier.*
Serves 6

1 recipe *Puff Pastry (page 248)*

4¼ *cups blackberries*

2 *tablespoons sugar*

1 *teaspoon framboise liqueur*

1 *recipe Tangerine Sabayon*
(page 245)

2 *cups Raspberry Sauce (page 251)*

3 *tablespoons powdered sugar*

On a lightly floured board, roll the puff
pastry ¹⁄₁₆ inch thick (see page 249 for rolling and cutting tips). Dock the puff pastry.
Cut into 12 pieces, each 4 by 5 inches.
Freeze the pastry for at least 1 hour.

Preheat the oven to 375 degrees.

Line 2 baking pans with parchment paper,
place the frozen puff pastry on the baking
pans, and cover with inverted wire mesh
baking racks. Bake for 15 to 20 minutes,
until golden brown.

Toss the berries, sugar, and liqueur in a
bowl. Put 1 piece of puff pastry on each
plate. Spoon on some of the berries and
then some of the sabayon. Drizzle on the
raspberry sauce. Sprinkle the remaining 6
pieces of puff pastry with powdered sugar
and place on top.

Sour Cherry Napoleons

*Dried sour cherries from Michigan are becoming a popular
ingredient and are now more readily available. They combine
beautifully with the liqueurs in the Basque Sabayon.*

Serves 6

4 cups dried sour cherries

2 cups freshly squeezed orange juice

1 cup water

1 tablespoon cornstarch

1 recipe Basque Sabayon (page
    245)

1 recipe Puff Pastry (page 248)

3 tablespoons powdered sugar

On a lightly floured board, roll the puff pastry $\frac{1}{16}$ inch thick (see page 249 for rolling and cutting tips). Dock the puff pastry. Cut it into 12 pieces, each 4 by 5 inches. Freeze the pastry for at least 1 hour.

Put the cherries, orange juice, and water in a saucepot. Cook over medium heat for about 10 minutes until cherries become plump.

Strain the cherries from the juice. Return all of the juice except $\frac{1}{2}$ cup to the pot. Whisk the cornstarch into the $\frac{1}{2}$ cup of liquid until it is incorporated and then whisk it into the rest of the cherry juice. Cook the liquid for about 5 minutes over medium heat until the sauce thickens.

Preheat the oven to 375 degrees.

Line 2 baking pans with parchment paper, place the frozen puff pastry on the baking pans, and cover with inverted wire mesh baking racks. Bake for approximately 15 minutes, until golden brown.

To assemble:
Put 1 piece of puff pastry on each of 6 plates. Put some of the cherries on top. Spoon some Basque sabayon over the cherries. Sprinkle the remaining 6 pieces of puff pastry with powdered sugar and place on top of the cherries. Serve at once.

Pear Napoleons
with Ginger Pastry Cream

*The perfume of ripe pears is universally cherished
and combines well with the spicy scent and bite of fresh ginger.*

Serves 6

8 ripe pears, peeled, cored, and
    sliced ⅓ inch thick

⅓ cup sugar

½ tablespoon freshly squeezed
    lemon juice

2 tablespoons brandy

Pinch salt

1 recipe Puff Pastry (page 248)

1 recipe Ginger Pastry Cream
    (page 239)

3 tablespoons powdered sugar

On a lightly floured board, roll the puff pastry ¹⁄₁₆ inch thick (see page 249 for rolling and cutting tips). Dock the puff pastry. Cut it into 12 pieces, each 4 by 5 inches. Freeze the pastry for at least 1 hour.

Put the pears, sugar, lemon juice, brandy, and salt in a 12-inch sauté pan. Cook over medium high heat until the pears are soft but still retain their shape, about 10 to 15 minutes. Set them aside until ready to serve the napoleons.

Preheat the oven to 375 degrees.

Line 2 baking pans with parchment paper, place the frozen puff pastry on the baking pans, and cover with inverted wire mesh baking racks. Bake for 15 to 20 minutes, until golden brown.

To assemble:
Put 1 piece of puff pastry on each plate. Spread about ¼ cup of ginger pastry cream on top of the puff pastry. Spoon some of the pears over the pastry cream. Dust 6 more pieces of puff pastry with powdered sugar and place over the pears. Serve immediately.

Almond Vacherin
with Bing Cherry Compote

This Bing cherry compote can be served by itself, over ice cream,
or in this case as a filling for meringue shells loaded with brandy cream.
Serves 8

Vacherins:

6 large egg whites

¾ cup plus 2 tablespoons sugar

½ cup powdered sugar

1 ounce sliced almonds, toasted and
*   finely ground*

A pastry bag with a ¼-inch plain
*   round tip*

Brandy Cream:

2 cups heavy whipping cream

¼ cup sugar

2 tablespoons brandy

To make the vacherins:
Preheat the oven to 200 degrees.

Put the egg whites in the bowl of an electric mixer. With the whisk attachment, whip them on medium speed until frothy. Increase to high speed and slowly add 2 tablespoons of granulated sugar. Continue to whip until soft peaks form. Slowly add ½ cup granulated sugar and continue whipping until stiff.

Mix together the remaining granulated sugar, the powdered sugar, and almonds. On low speed gently fold the nut-sugar mixture into the egg whites.

Line a sheet pan with parchment paper and "glue" the corners of the parchment onto the sheet pan with a little of the meringue.

Put a ½-inch plain round tip in a pastry bag. Pipe the meringue in a circular motion 3 inches in diameter, starting from the inside, to make a solid coil. When you get to the outside edge of the disk, continue to pipe out circles the width of the pastry tip on top of each other until you have created a 2-inch-high wall. Form 8 vacherins in the same manner. (You will have extra meringue so you can make a few extra and perfect your technique.)

Bake the meringues until they are dry and easily peel off the parchment paper, anywhere from several hours to overnight. Let them cool and serve them with the Bing cherry compote and brandy cream.

To make the brandy cream:
Put the cream with the sugar and brandy in a large stainless steel bowl. Whisk the cream until it holds its shape. Refrigerate the cream until ready to assemble the vacherins.

Bing Cherry Compote

8 cups Bing cherries, stemmed and pitted
¼ cup brandy
3 tablespoons Simple Syrup (page 250)
Pinch salt
3 ounces (¾ stick) sweet butter

★

To make the bing cherry compote:
Put the cherries in a large sauté pan with the brandy,
simple syrup, and salt. Cook over medium heat
for about 10 minutes until the cherries are soft
but still retain their shape.
Stir in the butter. Remove the cherries from the heat
and let them cool until they are just warm.

★

To serve, fill each vacherin one-half full
with the brandy cream and spoon the cherry compote in
and around the vacherin.

Frozen Desserts, Ice Creams, *and* Sorbets

4

People feel as passionately about ice cream and sorbet

as they do about politics. They will argue

with anyone over which flavor is best and whether a dense

or airy texture is preferred. At Stars our philosophy

on ice cream and sorbet is to use the best

and freshest ingredients possible. Ice cream and sorbet are

not only desserts by themselves but can be used

as starting points for other frozen desserts as well.

Peach Sorbet

The quality of this sorbet, as with all fruit sorbets, depends on
the ripeness of the fruit. White peaches would be best,
but any will do if well perfumed and right from the farmers' market.
Yield: 9 cups

16 ripe peaches (5½ pounds),
    pitted and sliced
2 cups Simple Syrup (page 250)
Pinch salt
2 teaspoons freshly squeezed
    lemon juice

Purée the peach slices in a food processor. Strain the purée through a medium-holed sieve to eliminate any small pieces of skin. There should be 6 cups of peach purée.

Pour the peach purée into a large bowl and add the simple syrup, lemon juice, and salt.

Freeze according to ice cream machine manufacturer's instructions.

Mango Sorbet

Serve with fresh berries.
Yield: 8 cups

9 ripe medium-sized mangoes,
    peeled and seeded
1 tablespoon freshly squeezed
    lemon juice
Pinch salt
2 cups Simple Syrup (page 250)

Place the mango pulp in a food processor. Purée the pulp and then strain the purée through a medium sieve. There should be about 4½ cups. Transfer the mango purée to a large bowl and add the other ingredients.

Freeze according to ice cream machine manufacturer's directions.

Apricot Sorbet

*The apricot season in California, although short, is very abundant.
Here's a great sorbet for the height of the apricot season.
Yield: 9 cups*

45 ripe apricots (5 pounds)

*Approximately 1¾ cups Simple
Syrup (page 250)*

*1 tablespoon freshly squeezed
lemon juice*

Pinch salt

Halve and pit the apricots. Purée them in a food processor. Strain the purée through a medium-holed sieve to eliminate any small pieces of skin. Place the apricot purée in a large bowl and add the other ingredients.

Freeze according to ice cream machine manufacturer's instructions.

Plum Sorbet

*Plums always produce a beautifully colored sorbet. The puréed skins
transfer just the right amount of color.
Yield: 7 cups*

25 ripe plums (4½ pounds), pitted

1¾ cups Simple Syrup (page 250)

Pinch salt

*1 teaspoon freshly squeezed
lemon juice*

Purée the plums in a food processor. Strain the plum purée through a medium sieve. There should be 4 cups of plum purée.

Place the plum purée in a large bowl and add the simple syrup, lemon juice, and salt.

Freeze according to ice cream machine manufacturer's instructions.

Pineapple Sorbet

One of Jeremiah's favorite desserts, and one for which he has a great nostalgia, is
from Escoffier: Peaches Rose Cheri. Nostalgic because of its white peaches and favorite because of its
pineapple ice (to say nothing of its sabayon and rose petals). Pineapple sorbet is among the best
because of its texture, which is perfect and easy to achieve.
Yield: about 2 quarts

3 ripe pineapples, peeled and cored

1½ cups Simple Syrup (page 250)

1½ teaspoons freshly squeezed
lemon juice

Pinch salt

Cut the pineapple into 2-inch pieces. Place the pieces in a food processor fitted with a metal blade. Purée the pineapple pieces and then strain them through a medium-holed sieve. There should be 6 cups of pineapple purée. Place the purée into a bowl and add the remaining ingredients.

Freeze according to ice cream machine manufacturer's instructions.

Cape Cod Cantaloupe Sorbet

From the nineteenth century high-living clambake days
on Cape Cod and Long Island.
Yield: 8 cups

6 pounds ripe cantaloupe, seeded

2 cups Simple Syrup (page 250)

4 teaspoons freshly squeezed
lemon juice

¼ teaspoon salt

¼ cup Malmsey Madeira

Remove the flesh of the cantaloupe from the rind and cut it into 3-inch pieces. Place the cantaloupe in a food processor fitted with the metal blade and purée. Place the purée in a large bowl and add the other ingredients.

Freeze according to ice cream machine manufacturer's instructions.

Ollalieberry Sorbet

This recipe is meant to be a model for any of the berry sorbets
excluding blueberry (for which the fruit must be cooked).
Yield: 8 cups

9 cups ollalieberries

2 teaspoons freshly squeezed
lemon juice

2½ cups Simple Syrup (page 250)

Pinch salt

Purée the ollalieberries in a food processor. Strain the purée through a medium-holed sieve to eliminate any seeds. There should be about 4½ cups of purée. In a large bowl, whisk the purée with the other ingredients.

Freeze according to ice cream machine manufacturer's instructions.

Strawberry Sorbet

As the strawberry season precedes that of all other berries,
enjoy this even in late spring.
Yield: 2 quarts

8 pints strawberries, hulled and
quartered

2 cups Simple Syrup (page 250)

2½ tablespoons freshly squeezed
lemon juice

Pinch salt

Purée the strawberries in a food processor. Strain the purée through a medium-holed sieve to eliminate any seeds. There should be about 6 cups of purée. Place the purée in a large bowl and add the other ingredients.

Freeze according to ice cream machine manufacturer's instructions.

Frozen Mandarins

This dessert was first served for a 1978 dinner in Big Sur to honor James Beard.
The guest list included Mr. and Mrs. James Nassikas (then of Stanford Court),
Marion Cunningham, Darryl Corti, Alice Walters, James and Dagmar Sullivan,
from Sacramento, and Cecilia Chiang. Jeremiah created this dessert
for Mrs. Chiang, calling it "Entrance of the Mandarins." The little oranges,
filled with their sorbet, were attached by gold wire to orange trees.
The trees were then wheeled out into the dining room and the mandarins served
tableside from the trees. Serve with Chinese Almond Cookies (page 194).

Serves 6

3⅓ cups strained mandarin
  orange juice (about 20 mandarin
  oranges)

1¾ cups Simple Syrup (page 250)

1½ teaspoons freshly squeezed
  lemon juice

Pinch salt

6 mandarin oranges

Place the orange juice in a large bowl. Stir in the Simple Syrup, lemon juice, and salt.

Freeze according to ice cream machine manufacturer's instructions.

Cut the tops off the mandarin oranges. Scoop out the inside pulp of the oranges. Freeze the oranges and the tops until hard.

Fill each frozen orange with the sorbet. Place the top on each orange. Freeze until ready to serve.

Frozen Kir Royale

*Framboise sorbet and Champagne sabayon are combined
to make a dessert out of the popular French aperitif. It is wonderful
served with Brown Butter Madeleines (page 199).*

Serves 6

12 cups raspberries

1 cup framboise liqueur

1 cup Simple Syrup (page 250)

1 teaspoon freshly squeezed
　　lemon juice

Pinch salt

1 recipe Champagne Sabayon
　　(page 245)

Purée the raspberries through a food mill fitted with a medium strainer. Strain the purée through a medium sieve to eliminate any seeds. You should have 3½ cups of purée. Place it in a bowl and add the framboise, simple syrup, lemon juice, and salt.

Freeze the sorbet according to ice cream machine manufacturer's instructions.

Serve the sorbet, topped with the Champagne sabayon, in beautiful tall glasses.

Frozen Sour Cherry Mousse

*Looking for a new frozen dessert, we added dried cherries
and toasted almonds to a sabayon and popped it in the freezer.
The result was delicious and has become a favorite at Stars.*
Makes about 8 cups

2 cups dried sour cherries

1 cup hot water

12 large egg yolks

¾ cup sugar

⅛ teaspoon salt

7½ tablespoons amaretto

7½ tablespoons freshly squeezed
   orange juice

1 tablespoon cassis

1½ cups heavy whipping cream

2 ounces sliced almonds

1 recipe Chantilly Cream
   (page 252)

Cover the sour cherries with the hot water and soak them for 15 minutes. Drain them and set them aside.

Place the egg yolks in a stainless steel bowl. Add the sugar and salt and whisk until incorporated. Stir in the amaretto, orange juice, and cassis.

Fill another bowl one quarter full of ice water and set aside.

Place the first bowl over a pot of simmering water and cook the mixture, whisking vigorously, for about 5 minutes, until thick.

Cool the egg mixture over the ice bath, whisking constantly.

Place the cream in the bowl of an electric mixer. With the whisk attachment, whip the cream on high speed until soft peaks form. Fold the cream, the cherries, and the almonds into the egg mixture. Freeze the mousse overnight. Serve in bowls with a dollop of chantilly cream.

Frozen Praline Mousse

Rich and creamy like ice cream, this frozen mousse doesn't require an ice cream machine.
Serve with warm Chocolate Sauce (page 237).
Yield: 1½ quarts

6 large eggs

1 cup sugar

Pinch salt

⅔ cup ground Praline (page 250)

1¾ cups heavy whipping cream

Whisk together the eggs, sugar, and salt in a large stainless steel mixing bowl. Place the bowl over a pot of simmering water and continuously whisk the mixture until very thick, about 10 minutes. Place the bowl over an ice bath and cool, whisking occasionally.

Place the praline in a food processor fitted with a metal blade. Finely grind the praline, using on-off pulses.

Place the cream in the bowl of an electric mixer. Using the whisk attachment, whip the cream on high speed until soft peaks form.

Fold the whipped cream and the ground praline into the cooled egg and sugar mixture. Freeze the mousse overnight before serving.

Espresso Granita

Granita is made without the use of an ice cream machine.
When served in tall stemmed glasses the icy crystals sparkle beautifully.
Biscotti (page 193) make an excellent accompaniment.
Yield: about 8 cups

8 cups cold espresso

3 cups superfine sugar

1 recipe Chantilly Cream

(page 252)

Pour the espresso into a large bowl. Stir in the sugar.

Pour the sweetened espresso into a shallow pan approximately 9 by 13 inches and place it in the freezer. Every half hour, roughly stir up the freezing mixture with the tines of a fork. This will give the granita a feathery and light icy texture.

Freeze the espresso until it is completely frozen, 8 hours to overnight, depending on your freezer.

Serve in tall glasses with chantilly cream and biscotti.

Pink Grapefruit-Champagne Granita

This is a light dessert to end any meal. It is not meant to be served with wine,
but to refresh. We prefer to use ruby grapefruit for their sweetness and color.
Serve with Russian Tea Cakes (page 198).
Yield: 10 cups

2 cups freshly squeezed pink
* grapefruit juice*
2 cups Champagne
1½ cups Simple Syrup (page 250)
Pinch salt

Pour the grapefruit juice in a large bowl. Add the remaining ingredients and whisk together. Pour the grapefruit mixture into a shallow pan approximately 9 by 13 inches and put in the freezer. Every half hour roughly stir up the freezing mixture with the tines of a fork. This will give the granita a feathery and light icy texture.

Freeze until the granita is completely frozen, 8 hours to overnight, depending on your freezer.

Sugar *and* Snow

*This dessert, created in honor of the maple syrup season, is based
on a local Vermont treat in which hot maple syrup is poured onto fresh Vermont snow
and eaten immediately. For those who have not had that pleasure, try this dessert.
Serve with Hazelnut Shortbread (page 203).*
Makes 1½ cups

1 cup sugar

¼ cup plus 1 tablespoon water

¾ cup pure maple syrup

3½ ounces sweet butter

6 scoops vanilla ice cream

Combine the sugar and ¼ cup of water in a heavy-bottomed saucepot. Dissolve the sugar over low heat. Increase the heat to high and cook the sugar until it is a golden-amber color. Slowly and very carefully stir in the maple syrup. Be cautious, as it will bubble when it is first added.

Stir in the butter and the remaining 1 tablespoon water.

Keep the sauce warm until ready to use or refrigerate it and reheat it in a double boiler.

To serve:
Scoop the vanilla ice cream into bowls and pour the warm maple sauce over the ice cream.

Chocolate Espresso Cream Sandwiches

*Meringues are by nature dry and brittle, but freezing them makes
their texture soft and chewy. We once served 3,000 "mini" versions of these
frozen cream sandwiches at a benefit for a local public television station.*

Serves 8

Espresso cream:

¾ *cup heavy whipping cream*

½ *pound mascarpone*

Pinch salt

1 tablespoon espresso grounds

2 tablespoons sugar

Chocolate Cream:

¾ *cup heavy whipping cream*

½ *pound mascarpone*

Pinch salt

*3 tablespoons cold Chocolate Sauce
(page 237)*

*16 Chocolate Meringue Shells
(page 247), piped into 3-inch
circles*

Powdered sugar for dusting

*1 recipe Vanilla Custard Sauce
(page 246)*

To make the espresso cream:
Place the cream and the mascarpone in a mixing bowl. Add the salt, espresso grounds, and sugar. Whisk until soft peaks form. Refrigerate the cream until ready to assemble the sandwiches.

To make the chocolate cream:
Place the cream and the mascarpone in a mixing bowl. Add the salt and chocolate sauce. Whisk until soft peaks form. Refrigerate the cream until ready to assemble the sandwiches.

To assemble the sandwiches:
Fill one pastry bag with the chocolate cream and a second pastry bag with the espresso cream. Pipe ¼ cup chocolate cream onto a meringue shell. Pipe the same amount of espresso cream on top of the chocolate cream. Place a second meringue shell on top of the espresso cream. Freeze the sandwiches for several hours to overnight. Serve with vanilla custard sauce. (If your freezer is very cold, let the sandwiches sit out at room temperature for 15 minutes before eating them. They should not be rock hard.)

Caramel Ice Cream

Two major rules for ice cream: First, it should be full of flavor, so that, for example, peach ice cream tastes like fresh peaches, caramel ice cream like caramel. You should not have to guess the flavor; it should be evident from the first bite. Second, the texture should be rich and smooth (the addition of milk prevents it from becoming too heavy).
Yield: 3 quarts

15 large egg yolks

½ teaspoon salt

½ cup water

2¼ cups sugar

4½ cups milk

4½ cups heavy whipping cream

Place the egg yolks in a large stainless steel mixing bowl. Add the salt and whisk until smooth. Set aside.

Combine the sugar and water in a heavy-bottomed saucepot large enough to eventually hold the milk and cream. Dissolve the sugar in the water over low heat. Increase to high heat and cook the syrup until it is a golden amber color. While the sugar is caramelizing, scald the milk and cream.

As soon as the caramel is a golden-amber color, slowly add the milk and cream, 2 tablespoons at a time. Be very careful, as the mixture will bubble up. Whisk the caramel cream into the eggs.

Strain and refrigerate the ice cream base until cold.

Freeze according to ice cream machine manufacturer's instructions.

Peach Ice Cream

I prefer puréed fruit in fruit ice cream, as pieces freeze and get too hard.
If you like, roughly chop or slice fresh peaches, toss them with sugar and a pinch of salt,
and place them on top of the ice cream before serving. Or serve with blueberry sauce.
Yield: about 2 quarts

8 large egg yolks

1 cup plus 2 tablespoons sugar

1 teaspoon salt

2¾ cups heavy whipping cream

2¼ cups milk

5½ pounds (about 14 large) ripe
   peaches, peeled and pitted

Place the egg yolks in a large stainless steel bowl. Add the sugar and salt and whisk until smooth. Set aside.

Place the cream and milk in a heavy-bottomed saucepot and bring to a boil. Slowly whisk the milk mixture into the egg yolk mixture. Strain and then refrigerate the ice cream base until cold.

Purée the peaches in a food processor. You should have 4¼ cups of purée. Whisk the peach purée into the cooled cream mixture.

Freeze according to ice cream machine manufacturer's instructions.

Rhubarb Ice Cream

Wonderful by itself, with Cornmeal Poundcake
(page 163), or with warm strawberries.
Yield: 2 quarts

8 cups rhubarb, chopped into
    ½-inch pieces

1½ cups sugar

½ cup water

¾ teaspoon salt

8 large egg yolks

2¼ cups milk

2¼ cups heavy whipping cream

A 2-inch piece vanilla bean

Combine the rhubarb with ½ cup of the sugar, the water, and ¼ teaspoon of the salt in a heavy-bottomed saucepot. Cook over medium heat, stirring occasionally, until the rhubarb is soft.

Place the rhubarb in a food processor fitted with the metal blade and purée it. Set the purée aside to cool.

Place the egg yolks in a large stainless steel bowl. Add the remaining 1 cup sugar and ½ teaspoon salt and whisk until smooth.

Place the milk and the cream in a heavy-bottomed saucepot. Add the vanilla bean and bring the milk-cream mixture to a boil. Slowly whisk it into the egg mixture.

Refrigerate the ice cream base until cold, and then strain it. Whisk the rhubarb purée into the ice cream base.

Freeze according to ice cream machine manufacturer's instructions.

Hazelnut Ice Cream

Serve with warm Chocolate and Caramel Sauces (pages 237 and 238).
Try substituting pecans for hazelnuts.
Yield: 2½ quarts

4¾ cups milk

5¼ cups heavy whipping cream

16 ounces hazelnuts, toasted,
   skinned, and coarsely chopped

18 large egg yolks

2¼ cups sugar

½ teaspoon salt

Place the milk and cream in a heavy-bottomed saucepot. Add the hazelnuts and scald the mixture. Remove the pot from the heat, cover, and let the hazelnuts steep in the milk for 15 minutes.

Whisk the egg yolks with the sugar and salt in a large mixing bowl. Bring the hazelnut milk back to a boil and slowly whisk it into the eggs.

Refrigerate the ice cream base until cold, and then strain it.

Freeze according to ice cream machine manufacturer's instructions.

Ginger Ice Cream

Serve with a drizzle of tropical flower honey
and Chinese Almond Cookies (page 194).
Makes about 2½ quarts

16 egg yolks

2¼ cups sugar

½ teaspoon salt

4½ cups milk

4½ cups heavy whipping cream

6 ounces fresh ginger root, cut into
1- to 1½-inch pieces.

Place the egg yolks in a large stainless steel bowl. Add the sugar and salt and whisk until smooth.

Place the milk and cream in a heavy-bottomed saucepot. Add the ginger and scald the milk mixture. Remove the pot from the heat, cover it, and allow the ginger to steep in the milk for 15 minutes. Bring the ginger milk to a boil and gradually whisk it into the egg yolk mixture.

Refrigerate the ice cream base until cold, and then strain it.

Freeze according to ice cream machine manufacturer's instructions.

Pumpkin Ice Cream

Incredible with hot Caramel or Chocolate Sauce (pages 238 and 237).
Yield: 2 quarts

8 large egg yolks

1 cup plus 2 tablespoons sugar

¼ teaspoon salt

2¼ cups milk

2¼ cups heavy whipping cream

1½ cups Pumpkin Purée

(page 241)

1 teaspoon ground cinnamon

¾ teaspoon ground ginger

Pinch freshly grated nutmeg

Place the egg yolks in a large stainless steel bowl. Add the sugar and salt and whisk until smooth. Set aside.

Place the milk and cream in a heavy-bottomed saucepot. Bring to a boil. Slowly whisk the milk mixture into the egg yolk mixture.

Refrigerate the ice cream base until cold and then strain.

Whisk the pumpkin purée, cinnamon, ginger, and nutmeg into the ice cream base.

Freeze according to ice cream machine manufacturer's instructions.

Raspberry Ice Cream

Serve with peaches that have been lightly tossed in brown sugar.
Yield: 2 quarts

6 cups raspberries

8 large egg yolks

1 cup sugar

¼ teaspoon salt

2¼ cups milk

2¼ cups heavy whipping cream

Purée the raspberries in a food processor. Pass the purée through a medium sieve to eliminate the seeds. There should be 1½ cups of raspberry purée.

Place the egg yolks in a large stainless steel bowl. Whisk in the sugar and salt.

Place the milk and cream in a heavy-bottomed saucepot and bring to a boil. Slowly pour the milk mixture into the egg mixture.

Refrigerate the ice cream base until cold, and then strain.

Stir the raspberry purée into the ice cream base.

Freeze according to ice cream machine manufacturer's instructions.

White Chocolate-Espresso Parfait

We incorporated some Amaretto di Saronno in the sauce for
this white chocolate parfait to round out and jazz up the espresso flavor.
Serve topped with crushed amaretti for some added crunch.
Serves 6

White chocolate ice cream:

18 ounces white chocolate,
*   finely chopped*

12 large egg yolks

1⅔ cups sugar

Pinch salt

3¼ cups milk

3½ cups heavy whipping cream

Espresso-Amaretto Sauce:

1¼ cups cold espresso

½ cup Amaretto di Saronno

1½ cups Chantilly Cream
*   (page 252)*

1 cup bittersweet chocolate shavings

½ cup crushed amaretti cookies

To make the ice cream:
Put the white chocolate in a stainless steel bowl. Place the bowl over a pot of simmering water and melt the chocolate, whisking until it is completely smooth and no pieces remain. Turn off the heat, but keep the bowl over the water to keep the chocolate warm.

Place the yolks in a large stainless steel bowl. Add the sugar and salt and whisk until smooth. Place the milk and cream in a heavy-bottomed saucepot. Scald the milk mixture and slowly whisk it into the egg mixture.

Stir in the reserved white chocolate.

Strain and refrigerate the ice cream base until cold.

Freeze according to ice cream machine manufacturer's instructions.

Espresso-Amaretto Sauce:
Combine the espresso and the amaretto in a pitcher.

To serve:
Pour a little of the espresso-amaretto sauce in the bottom of six tall glasses. Scoop some white chocolate ice cream into the glasses and pour more of the sauce over the ice cream. Top with chantilly cream, shaved chocolate, and crushed amaretti.

Profiteroles *with* Caramel Ice Cream *and* Warm Cocoa Sauce

In France I was served profiteroles with warm chocolate sauce in the most decadent manner:
As a plate of profiteroles and ice cream was placed in front of me, the waiter hovered with
a silver pitcher, eighteen inches tall, full of hot cocoa sauce. He poured until I said stop, which,
since I was so mesmerized by the entire process, was about 5 minutes later!
Serves 8

1 cup water

Pinch salt

2 ounces (½ stick) sweet butter

1½ teaspoons sugar

1 cup flour

4 large eggs

1 recipe Vanilla Custard Sauce
   (page 246)

1 recipe Caramel Ice Cream
   (page 116)

A pastry bag fitted with ½-inch
   plain tip

Preheat the oven to 375 degrees.

Combine the water, salt, butter, and sugar in a heavy-bottomed saucepan. Bring the mixture to a boil.

Remove the pot from the heat and stir in the flour, mixing well. Return the pot to the stove and cook over medium heat until the dough begins to come away clean from the sides of the pan. This will take a couple of minutes.

Place the dough in the bowl of an electric mixer and let it cool for 3–5 minutes.

Add the eggs, one at a time, with the paddle attachment on medium speed, beating well after each addition.

Place the mixture in a pastry bag fitted with a ½-inch tip. Pipe out 24 profiteroles, each about 1 inch across and 1½ inches high.

Bake the profiteroles for 25 to 30 minutes, until golden brown. Turn off the oven. Make a small slice in each profiterole and return them to the oven, leaving the door ajar. Leave the profiteroles in the oven for about 10 to 15 minutes, allowing the insides to dry out almost completely.

To serve:
Cut each profiterole in half. Spoon some vanilla custard sauce on the bottom of each plate. Place the bottom halves of 3 profiteroles on the plate and scoop the caramel ice cream on top of each one. Cover with the top halves of the profiteroles. Pour the warm cocoa sauce over the profiteroles at the table. You can either do this from a large pitcher or give each person his own individual pitcher.

Warm Cocoa Sauce for the Profiteroles

*

Yield: 1¾ cups
½ cup plus 2 tablespoons cocoa powder
1¾ cups water
1 cup sugar
6 tablespoons (¾ stick) sweet butter
2 tablespoons heavy whipping cream

*

To make the cocoa sauce:
Mix the cocoa powder with ½ cup of the water
in a large bowl to make a thick paste.

Place the remaining 1¼ cups water
and the sugar in a heavy-bottomed saucepot
and bring to a boil.
Stir into the cocoa paste.

Transfer the cocoa mixture back to the pot and simmer,
stirring occasionally, for approximately 15 minutes,
until it thickens enough to coat the back of a metal spoon.
Cool slightly and then whisk in the butter and cream.

Serve warm.
This sauce can be reheated in a double boiler.

Pies, Tarts, *and* Puff Pastry

5

*

Superb doughs and puff pastry

are the backbone of desserts. A homey pie, a delicate tart,

or a sophisticated napoleon, however wonderful the filling,

is a major disappointment if it does not have a crust

that melts in your mouth. Pay attention

to the basic rules of pastry making and you will succeed

in making light and flaky crusts and puff pastry:

Do not overmix the dough and be careful not to add

too much water as both of these will make the crust tough.

Pies, tarts, and baked puff pastry are best eaten

the day they are made.

*

Macaroon Nut Tart

This was designed for the tropical theme of Jeremiah's Restaurant 690 in San Francisco.
The coconut gives a new sparkle to the traditional nut tart.
Serves 6 to 8

1 cup sweetened shredded coconut

2½ ounces sweet butter

½ cup firmly packed light brown
   sugar

4 large egg yolks

1 teaspoon almond extract

Pinch salt

⅓ cup unsweetened coconut milk

3 ounces toasted macadamia nuts,
   cut in half

1 ounce toasted pecans

1 partially baked 9-inch tart shell
   (page 240)

Preheat the oven to 325 degrees.

Spread the coconut on a baking sheet and toast it for about 10 minutes, until it is light brown.

Increase the oven temperature to 350 degrees.

Melt the butter in a small saucepot and stir in the brown sugar.

Put the egg yolks in a large bowl. Stir in the almond extract, coconut milk, and salt. Whisk in the butter mixture. Add the coconut, macadamia nuts, and pecans. Pour the nut filling into the tart shell and smooth the surface with a spatula.

Bake the tart for about 20 minutes, until the tart is golden brown and just set.

Serve the tart warm or at room temperature.

Bing Cherry Tart

All you need for this dessert are roadside summer cherries. Be sure to buy extra cherries
so you have some to snack on while you are baking the tart.
Serves 6 to 8

5½ cups Bing cherries

½ cup plus 1 teaspoon sugar

2 tablespoons tapioca flour

1 teaspoon freshly squeezed
    lemon juice

Pinch salt

¼ teaspoon almond extract

1 prebaked 9-inch tart shell
    (page 240)

10 strips lattice (page 240)

Preheat the oven to 350 degrees.

Stem and pit the cherries. There should be 4 cups of pitted cherries. Place the cherries in a pot. Cover the pot and cook the cherries over medium-low heat until they begin to give off some of their juice. Add ½ cup sugar, tapioca flour, lemon juice, salt, and almond extract. Continue to cook, uncovered, just until the liquid starts to thicken.

Cool the cherry mixture to room temperature.

Spread the cherries in the tart shell. Arrange the lattice in a crosshatch pattern over the tart. Sprinkle the remaining 1 teaspoon of sugar over the lattice.

Bake the tart for 15 to 20 minutes, until the lattice is golden.

Serve the cherry tart warm or at room temperature.

Apple Cinnamon Custard Tart

The custard in this tart keeps the apples juicy and adds a creamy texture.
Serves 6 to 8

1 egg white

1 prebaked 9-inch tart shell

    (page 240)

1 large egg

2 large egg yolks

6 tablespoons sugar

1 cup heavy whipping cream

½ teaspoon ground cinnamon

Pinch salt

3 or 4 apples, juicy and not too firm

    variety, peeled and sliced

    ¹⁄₁₆ inch thick

Preheat the oven to 325 degrees.

Lightly beat the egg white in a small bowl and brush a thin layer on the bottom of the tart shell. Bake the crust for 5 minutes to seal it.

In a mixing bowl, whisk together the egg, egg yolks, and sugar. Add the cream, cinnamon, and salt. Set aside.

Arrange the apples in the tart shell, slightly overlapping, in a circular pattern. Carefully pour the custard over the apples until the tart is full. (There may be extra custard depending on the height of the sides of the tart shell.)

Bake the tart for 10 minutes. Press the apples down with a large spatula so they are covered with the custard. Be careful when you do this not to destroy the circular pattern of the apples. Bake the tart for an additional 15 minutes, until the custard is set but not completely firm in the center.

Let the tart cool to room temperature before serving.

Lemon Mascarpone Cream Tart
with Figs *and* Raspberries

The lemon cream filling is a nice light accent for the fruit.
Tossing the fruit in the liqueur gives the tart a pretty glaze.
Serves 6 to 8

3 large eggs

5 tablespoons freshly squeezed
    lemon juice

6 tablespoons heavy cream

Pinch salt

1 teaspoon chopped lemon zest

3 ounces cream cheese

2 ounces mascarpone

¼ cup sugar

1 prebaked 9-inch tart shell
    (page 240)

8 to 10 black mission figs, cut into
    ½-inch slices

1 cup raspberries

¼ cup cassis liqueur

Preheat the oven to 325 degrees.

Combine the eggs, lemon juice, cream,
salt, lemon zest, cream cheese, mascarpone,
and sugar in a bowl of an electric mixer.
Using the whisk attachment, whisk the mixture on medium speed until smooth.

Skim any bubbles off the top of the mixture.
Pour the lemon cream into the tart shell.

Bake the tart for 20 to 25 minutes, until set.

When the tart is cool, gently combine the
figs and raspberries with the cassis liqueur
and neatly arrange them on top of the tart.

The tart should be served the same day
it is made.

Blackberry Streusel Tart

This tart is wonderful on a cool summer night when made with juicy
perfectly ripe blackberries and served with a big dollop of chantilly cream.
Or serve it warm with a scoop of Raspberry Ice Cream (page 122).
Serves 6 to 8

Streusel:

¾ cup flour

⅓ cup firmly packed brown sugar

Pinch salt

3 ounces (¾ stick) cold sweet butter

Tart Filling:

3 cups blackberries

½ cup sugar

1 tablespoon tapioca flour

½ teaspoon freshly squeezed
    lemon juice

1 prebaked 9-inch tart shell
    (page 240)

1 recipe Chantilly Cream
    (page 252)

Preheat the oven to 350 degrees.

Combine all of the streusel ingredients in a food processor fitted with the metal blade. With pulsing switches, process until the butter is the size of large peas. Set aside.

For the tart filling:
In a mixing bowl, gently combine the blackberries, sugar, tapioca flour, and lemon juice. Spread the blackberry mixture evenly in the tart shell.

Sprinkle the streusel over the tart.

Bake the tart for 20 minutes, until the streusel is browned and the fruit is bubbling.

Cool the tart for at least 15 minutes before cutting.

Chocolate Truffle Tart

*Terribly rich, like one of those perfect truffles from (the late) Mary's
in Paris, to be savored in small heavenly slices.*
Serves 6 to 8

½ plus ⅓ cup heavy whipping cream

3½ ounces bittersweet chocolate,
   finely chopped

1 prebaked tart shell (page 240)

3 tablespoons sweet butter

½ cup firmly packed dark brown
   sugar

¼ cup sugar

1 teaspoon vanilla extract

2 ounces toasted, skinned, and
   coarsely chopped hazelnuts

½ recipe Vanilla Pastry Cream
   (page 239)

Put the ½ cup cream in a small saucepot and bring it to a boil. Remove it from the heat and add the chopped chocolate. Let the chocolate cream stand for 5 minutes and then whisk it until smooth. Cool to lukewarm and pour it into the bottom of the tart shell. Refrigerate for 30 minutes until the chocolate cream is almost set.

Melt the butter in another small saucepot and stir in the brown and granulated sugars. Cook over medium-low heat for 5 minutes. Stir in the remaining ⅓ cup cream and the vanilla extract and continue to cook the mixture for another 5 minutes. Remove from the stove and stir in the hazelnuts. Cool to room temperature.

Spread the pastry cream over the chocolate layer and then top with the hazelnut mixture, being careful not to mix the two together.

Refrigerate the tart for 30 minutes. Take it out of the refrigerator 15 minutes before serving it.

Mango Lime Mousse Tart

In this tropical fruit tart, the sweetness of the mangoes balances nicely
with the tart lime flavor of the mousse.
Serves 6 to 8

3 large eggs

3 large egg yolks

¾ cup sugar

½ cup plus 1 tablespoon freshly
squeezed lime juice

1 prebaked 9-inch tart shell
(page 240)

3 ripe mangoes, peeled, pitted, and
thinly sliced

1 tablespoon dark rum

1 recipe Chantilly Cream
(page 252)

Combine the eggs, egg yolks, and sugar in a stainless steel bowl. Whisk in the lime juice.

Set the bowl over a pot of simmering water and whisk the lime mixture continually for about 5 minutes, until it is thick and mounds slightly. Remove the bowl from the stove and let the lime mousse cool for 5 minutes, stirring occasionally.

Pour the mousse into the tart shell. Refrigerate the tart for about 1 hour, until the filling is set.

Toss the mangoes gently in the rum. Arrange the mangoes in the tart shell, slightly overlapping, in a circular pattern.

Refrigerate the tart until ready to serve. Serve with chantilly cream.

Cornmeal Tartlets *with* Orange Crème Fraîche *and* Strawberries

The tanginess of the crème fraîche, the sweetness of the strawberries,
and the crunchiness of the cornmeal make for a wonderful combination.
Yield: 6 tartlets

Cornmeal Tarts:

1 cup cornmeal

1 cup flour

1 teaspoon salt

3 tablespoons sugar

2 teaspoons baking powder

3 ounces (¾ stick) cold sweet butter

¾ cup heavy whipping cream

Orange Crème Fraîche:

2 cups Crème Fraîche (page 253)

1 teaspoon chopped orange zest

1½ tablespoons freshly squeezed
   orange juice

Pinch salt

1 tablespoon sugar

3 pints strawberries, hulled and
   sliced

1 tablespoon sugar

1 recipe Strawberry Sauce
   (page 251)

Six 4½-inch tartlet shells with
   removable bottoms

To make the tarts:
Preheat the oven to 325 degrees.

Put the cornmeal, flour, salt, sugar, and baking powder in the bowl of an electric mixer. Using the paddle attachment on low speed, mix in the butter until it is the size of small peas. Continue to mix and slowly add the cream just until the dough comes together.

On a lightly floured board, roll out the dough ⅛ inch thick.

Cut the dough into six 5-inch circles. Line the tart shells with the dough and refrigerate them for 30 minutes. Line the shells with parchment paper and fill with pie weights or uncooked rice kernels. Bake for 15 minutes. Remove the paper and weights and bake the tarts for 10 minutes more.

To make the orange crème fraîche:
Put the crème fraîche, orange zest, orange juice, salt, and sugar in the bowl of an electric mixer. Using the whisk attachment, whip on medium high speed until thick. Refrigerate the cream until ready to serve the tarts.

To serve:
Put the strawberries in a bowl and gently mix in the sugar.

Fill the tarts with the orange cream. Top with the strawberries and drizzle on some of the strawberry sauce.

French Apple Tartlets

*In Paris, at irregular intervals throughout the day,
one can buy at the famous bakery Poilane the best apple tartlets,
coming right out of the oven. The locals line up for them
(in the neighborhood they seem to sense the schedule).
These are modeled after those made by Poilane.
They can be reheated but they are better eaten right out of the oven.*

Serves 8

1 recipe *Puff Pastry (page 248)*

7 *firm, juicy apples, peeled, cored,
     and sliced ⅛ inch thick*

¾ *cup sugar*

2 *ounces (½ stick) sweet butter*

¼ *teaspoon salt*

1 *tablespoon calvados*

2 *tablespoons freshly squeezed
     lemon juice*

1 *cup Crème Fraîche (page 253)*

On a lightly floured board, roll out the puff pastry into a rectangle ⅛ inch thick. Cut it into 5-inch squares. (See puff pastry recipe for cutting tips.) Carefully transfer the squares of puff pastry onto a baking sheet, making sure that they are not touching each other. Freeze the puff pastry for at least 1 hour, until frozen.

Put the apples in a large pan with the sugar, butter, salt, calvados, and lemon juice. Cook them gently over medium heat, stirring often, until they are soft. Transfer the apples to a bowl and let them cool to room temperature.

Preheat the oven to 375 degrees. Remove the puff pastry from the freezer and allow it to thaw at room temperature until it is malleable, about 15 minutes. Place ½ cup of the cooked apples in the middle of each square. Fold the 4 corners over the apples in toward the center of the tart.

Bake the tarts for about 30 minutes, until golden brown. Serve them warm with the crème fraîche.

Pear Frangipane Tart

This tart served warm with chantilly cream is a fall favorite.
You can substitute plums or apricots for the pears.
Serves 6 to 8

Frangipane:

4 ounces toasted sliced almonds

2 ounces (½ stick) soft sweet butter

1½ teaspoons brandy

⅓ cup sugar

1 large egg

Brandy butter:

2 ounces (½ stick) sweet butter

1¼ teaspoons brandy

1 teaspoon freshly squeezed
  lemon juice

2 teaspoons sugar

1 prebaked 9-inch tart shell
  (page 240)

7 ripe pears, peeled, cored, and
  sliced ⅛ inch thick

1 recipe Chantilly Cream
  (page 252)

Preheat the oven to 350 degrees.

To make the frangipane:
Put the almonds, butter, brandy, and sugar in the bowl of an electric mixer. With the paddle attachment, beat on medium speed for 2 minutes, until the almonds are broken up and the butter is creamed. Mix in the egg. Set aside.

To make the brandy butter:
Combine the butter, brandy, lemon juice, and sugar in a small pot. Cook over low heat until the butter is melted and the sugar is dissolved.

Spread the almond frangipane on the bottom of the tart shell. Arrange the pears in the shell, slightly overlapping, in a circular pattern. Brush half of the brandy butter on top of the pears.

Bake the tart for about 25 minutes, until the pears are golden brown at the edges. Remove it from the oven and brush the top of the tart with the remaining brandy butter.

Serve the tart warm or at room temperature, with the chantilly cream.

Pistachio Pithiviers

*Pithiviers: grandest of all puff pastry desserts, unmatched in stature
when perfectly made. Here it is given a wonderful twist with pistachios instead of
the traditional almonds. Serve warm with Double Cream (page 252).*

Serves 6

3 ounces toasted pistachios

¼ cup flour

5 ounces (1¼ sticks) soft sweet
    butter

¾ cup powdered sugar

1 teaspoon chopped lemon zest

2 large eggs

1 recipe Puff Pastry (page 248)

1 recipe Double Cream (page 252)

Preheat the oven to 375 degrees.

Put the pistachios and the flour in a food processor fitted with the metal blade and grind finely.

Put the butter and sugar in the bowl of an electric mixer. Using the paddle attachment, cream the butter and the sugar for 2 minutes, until light and fluffy. Add the ground pistachios and the lemon zest and mix until combined. Add 1 egg. Refrigerate the pistachio butter for several hours until firm.

Cut the puff pastry in half and put half in the refrigerator. On a lightly floured board, roll out the pastry ⅛ inch thick. Cut it into six 3½-inch circles. Refrigerate the circles while you roll out the other half of the dough.

On a lightly floured board, roll out the remaining puff pastry ⅛ inch thick. Cut it into six 4½-inch circles.

In a small bowl, lightly beat the remaining egg.

Place about 2 tablespoons of the pistachio mixture in the middle of each of the 3½-inch circles. Brush the outer rim of the circles with the beaten egg. Cover the pistachio mixture with the 4½-inch circles. Press the rims of the two circles together to seal. Refrigerate the pithiviers for ½ hour.

Press a fork along the edges of the pithiviers to seal. Score a decorative pattern with a very sharp paring knife on the top of each pithiviers, being careful not to cut completely through the pastry. Make a small vent hole in each center. Brush the tops of the pithiviers with remaining beaten egg.

Bake the pithiviers for 15–20 minutes until golden brown.

Serve the pithiviers warm with double cream.

Cranberry Linzertorte

*A fall version of raspberry linzertorte, this one is a nice surprise —
something different for the holiday season.*
Serves 6 to 8

Crust:

1 cup flour

6 tablespoons sugar

Pinch ground cloves

½ teaspoon ground cinnamon

*3½ ounces sliced almonds, toasted
and finely chopped*

1 cooked egg yolk, finely sieved

2 raw egg yolks

1 teaspoon vanilla extract

¼ teaspoon almond extract

*6 ounces (1½ sticks) soft sweet
butter*

½ teaspoon chopped lemon zest

Cranberry Filling:

5 cups cranberries

1 cup plus 1 tablespoon sugar

1 tablespoon chopped orange zest

3 tablespoons water

To make the crust:
Combine the flour, sugar, cloves, cinnamon, chopped almonds, and the cooked egg yolk in the bowl of an electric mixer. With the paddle attachment beat in the raw egg yolks on medium speed. Stir in the vanilla and almond extracts. Add the butter and lemon zest and mix until smooth.

Reserve one-third of the dough for the lattice. Press the remaining dough into the sides and bottom of a 9-inch tart shell. It should be ¼ inch thick. Divide the reserved lattice dough into 8 equal portions. By hand, roll each piece into a 9-inch strip the width of a pencil. Refrigerate the tart shell and the lattice for at least 1 hour until firm.

To make the cranberry filling:
Combine cranberries, sugar, orange zest, and water in a nonaluminum pot. Cook over medium heat, stirring occasionally, for about 15 minutes, until the cranberries are soft. Cool to room temperature.

Preheat the oven to 350 degrees.

Fill the tart shell with the cooled cranberry filling and arrange the lattice on top in a crosshatch pattern. Trim the edges of the lattice so they do not hang over the edge of the tart.

Bake the linzertorte for 30 to 35 minutes, until the shell and lattice are golden brown and the filling is bubbly.

Serve the linzertorte at room temperature.

Plum Pie

Plum pie has to be my favorite type of pie.
Not often seen, it is imaginative yet still gives all the comfort that
pies should give. Serve it with Hazelnut Ice Cream (page 119)
for a heartwarming combination.
Serves 8 to 10

⅓ cup water

1½ cups plus 1 tablespoon sugar

8 cups ½-inch-thick slices ripe, firm

    plums (about 20 plums)

¼ cup cornstarch

¼ cup brandy

Pinch salt

2 teaspoons freshly squeezed

    lemon juice

4 ounces (1 stick) sweet butter

1 partially baked 10-inch pie shell

    (page 240)

1 recipe lattice (page 240)

Preheat the oven to 350 degrees.

Bring the water and 1½ cups of the sugar to a boil in a heavy-bottomed nonaluminum pot large enough to eventually hold the plums.

Add half the sliced plums to the pot and return the liquid to a boil.

Stir together the cornstarch and the brandy in a small bowl. Add the brandy-cornstarch mixture, salt, and lemon juice to the pot. Gently stir in the butter and the rest of the plums, being careful not to break up the plums.

Spoon the plums into the partially baked pie shell with a slotted spoon. (You will not need the leftover liquid.) Arrange the lattice in a crosshatch pattern over the pie. Sprinkle the remaining 1 tablespoon sugar on top of the lattice.

Bake the pie for 35 to 40 minutes, until it is set. Let it cool for at least 30 minutes before serving.

Pumpkin Pie

Since everyone eats pumpkin pie on Thanksgiving, why not make it the best?
It's the addition of the rum and the heavy cream that does it in this recipe, which comes
from Carolyn Weil, the first pastry chef at Stars.
Serves 8 to 10

3 large eggs

½ cup firmly packed light brown

    sugar

½ cup Karo syrup

1½ cups heavy whipping cream

1½ cups Pumpkin Purée (page

    241)

1 tablespoon rum

½ teaspoon salt

1 teaspoon ground cinnamon

¾ teaspoon ground ginger

1 partially baked 10-inch pie shell

    (page 240)

1 recipe Chantilly Cream

    (page 252)

Preheat the oven to 350 degrees.

Whisk together the eggs and the brown sugar in a large mixing bowl. Add the Karo syrup and whisk until smooth. Stir in the cream, pumpkin purée, and rum. Add the salt, cinnamon, and ginger and mix until incorporated. Pour the mixture into the pie shell.

Bake the pie for about 30 minutes, until set. Cool the pie to room temperature and then serve with chantilly cream.

Maple Pecan Pie

Pecan pie can all too often be ordinary,
but the use of maple syrup turns this one into a classic Stars dessert,
especially served warm with coffee ice cream. Total sin.
Serves 8 to 10

4 large eggs

⅔ cup sugar

½ cup maple syrup

½ cup Karo syrup

3 ounces (¾ stick) sweet butter,
  melted

12 ounces coarsely chopped and
  toasted pecans (3½ cups)

1 partially baked 10-inch pie shell
  (page 240)

1 recipe Chantilly Cream
  (page 252)

Preheat the oven to 325 degrees.

Whisk together the eggs and sugar in a large mixing bowl. Stir in the maple and Karo syrups and then the melted butter.

Put the pecans in the pie shell and slowly pour in the syrup.

Bake the pie for 20 to 25 minutes, until the surface of the pie is cracked and the filling is just set.

Serve the pie warm or at room temperature with ice cream or chantilly cream.

Banana Cream Pie

*A great banana cream pie should be full of bananas
with just enough pastry cream to hold them together,
all topped with a thick layer of crème fraîche.*
Serves 8 to 10

5 medium bananas, peeled and
   sliced ⅛ inch thick

1 teaspoon dark rum

1 teaspoon freshly squeezed
   lime juice

1 recipe Brown Sugar Pastry
   Cream (page 239)

1 prebaked 10-inch pie shell
   (page 240)

¾ cup Crème Fraîche (page 253)

1 cup sour cream

1 cup Chocolate Sauce (page 237)

Toss the bananas with the rum and lime juice in a mixing bowl.

Spread about ¾ cup of the pastry cream in the bottom of the pie shell. Place the bananas evenly on top and cover with the remaining pastry cream.

Put the crème fraîche in the bowl of an electric mixer. With the whisk attachment whip on medium high speed until thick. Place the sour cream in a separate bowl and whisk it until it is smooth. Add the crème fraîche to the sour cream and fold them together.

Top the pie with the cream and refrigerate it until ready to serve. Serve with warm chocolate sauce drizzled over the top.

Bitter Lemon Pie

*With their unique flavor, sweetness, and tender skins, Meyer lemons
are superb for this pie. If you don't have them, any thin-skinned lemons will do —
but be sure to use an additional 2 tablespoons of sugar. Serve warm with vanilla ice cream.*
Serves 8 to 10

*2 large Meyer lemons, sliced paper-
thin, halved, and seeded*

2 cups plus 2 tablespoons sugar

3 large eggs

½ cup freshly squeezed lemon juice

*1 partially baked 10-inch pie shell
(page 240)*

*1 10-inch top shell, unbaked
(page 240)*

2 tablespoons heavy whipping cream

Preheat the oven to 375 degrees.

Toss the lemons and 2 cups of the sugar together in a large mixing bowl. Let them sit for 15 minutes.

Lightly whisk the eggs together in a separate bowl. Stir them into the lemons. Add the lemon juice. Place the lemon mixture in the pie shell.

Cover the pie with the top shell, sealing the top and bottom shells together. Fold the edge of the top shell under the rim of the bottom shell and crimp the edges to seal them.

Brush the top of the pie with the cream and sprinkle the remaining 2 tablespoons of sugar over it. Make several small vents in the top crust to let steam escape while the pie is baking.

Bake the pie for 20 minutes. Reduce the heat to 350 degrees and bake the pie for 35 minutes more, until the filling is thick and bubbly. If the pie gets brown before the filling has finished baking, cover it with foil. Cool the pie for at least 30 minutes before cutting.

Praline Mocha Napoleons

An updated version of the classic napoleon.
It is necessary to assemble this dessert at the last minute
to make sure that the puff pastry remains crisp.

Serves 6

1 recipe *Puff Pastry (page 248)*

1 cup sugar

⅓ cup water

2 ounces sliced almonds

1 recipe *Espresso Pastry Cream*

(page 239)

1 recipe *Chocolate Custard Sauce*

(page 246)

On a lightly floured board, roll the puff pastry ¹⁄₁₆ inch thick (see puff pastry recipe on page 248 for rolling and cutting tips). Dock the puff pastry. Cut it into 18 pieces, each 4 by 5 inches. Put the pieces on a sheet pan lined with parchment paper. (You can stack them between sheets of parchment paper.) Freeze the puff pastry for at least 1 hour.

Preheat the oven to 375 degrees.

Line baking pans with parchment paper, put the frozen puff pastry on the baking pans, and cover with inverted wire mesh baking racks. Bake the pastry for 15 to 20 minutes, until golden brown.

For the praline tops:
Dissolve the sugar in the water in a heavy-bottomed saucepan over low heat. Increase the heat to high and cook the sugar until it is a golden amber color. Stir in the almonds. Be careful, as the caramel is very hot. Working quickly with a pastry brush, brush a thin layer of caramel on top of 8 pieces of the puff pastry. (Do not make the caramel layer too thick or the puff pastry will be hard to eat.) Set the caramel tops aside to cool. These will be the top layers of the napoleons.

To assemble the napolcons:
Place a piece of puff pastry on each plate and top with 2–3 tablespoons of the pastry cream. Spoon some of the chocolate custard sauce over the pastry cream. Place another piece of puff pastry on the custard sauce and spoon on more pastry cream. Finish the napoleon with a piece of the caramelized puff.

Serve immediately.

Cakes

6

*

Cakes should not only be thought of

as two-layer cakes with frosting. These types of cakes,

although they are old favorites, are better suited

eaten by themselves in the middle of the afternoon or late at night.

At Stars we have expanded the definition of cakes.

They can be light and delicate or rich and decadent.

With the addition of creams, sauces, and fruits, cakes

are vitalized into full-fledged desserts,

appropriate as the final course of any meal.

*

Pumpkin Cheesecake

An alternative to pumpkin pie on Thanksgiving, particularly good with a little
Chocolate Sauce (page 237) drizzled over it. Be sure to use cream cheese without additives,
as the flavor and texture of the cake will be smoother and creamier.
Serves 10 to 12

Crust:

2 cups finely ground Ginger
*   Cookie crumbs (see page 190)*

3 tablespoons melted sweet butter

Cheesecake:

1 pound 13 ounces cream cheese

1 cup plus 2 tablespoons sugar

Pinch salt

2 large eggs

¼ teaspoon ground ginger

½ teaspoon ground cinnamon

1¾ cups Pumpkin Purée
*   (page 241)*

9 ounces mascarpone

A 9-inch springform pan

Preheat the oven to 300 degrees.

To make the crust:
Put the cookie crumbs in a small bowl and stir in the melted butter. Press the mixture in the bottom of the springform pan. Bake the crust for 10 minutes.

To make the cheesecake:
Put the cream cheese in the bowl of an electric mixer. Using the paddle attachment, beat on medium speed for about 2 minutes, until smooth. Continuing to mix, slowly add the sugar and the salt.

Add the eggs 1 at a time and mix well. Add the ginger, cinnamon, and pumpkin purée. Decrease to low speed and stir in the mascarpone. Spread the batter over the cooked crust.

Put the cheesecake in the oven. Put a pan of hot water on another rack below the cake. (The steam prevents a crust from forming on top of the cake.) Bake the cheesecake for 35 to 60 minutes, until almost set. (The center of the cake will not be completely firm.)

When the cake is done, loosen it from the edges of the pan by running a knife around the inside edge. Let the cake cool for 30 minutes at room temperature. Both these steps help prevent the top from cracking. Refrigerate the cheesecake in its pan until cold.

Unmold the cheesecake by running a knife around the inside edge of the pan.

To serve the cheesecake, cut it with a hot dry knife. (Dip the knife in hot water and then dry it off.)

Ginger Mascarpone Cheesecake
with a Chocolate Crust

What makes this a very special cheesecake is the richness of the mascarpone
and the fresh cream cheese (without any additives), which gives it a light texture.
Add a chocolate crust and you have a beauty.
Serves 10 to 12

Cheesecake:

2 pounds cream cheese

½ pound mascarpone

1¼ cups sugar

2 large eggs

1½ tablespoons fresh grated
*   ginger root*

Prepare crust (see opposite)

To make the cheesecake:
Preheat the oven to 300 degrees.

Put the cream cheese and the mascarpone in the bowl of an electric mixer. Using the paddle attachment, beat on medium speed until smooth. Continuing to mix, slowly add the sugar.

Beat in the eggs one at a time, mixing well after each addition. Stir in the grated ginger. Spread the batter over the baked crust.

Put the cheesecake in the oven. Place a pan of hot water on another rack below the cheesecake. (The steam from the water prevents a crust from forming on the top of the cake.)

Bake the cheesecake for 35 to 60 minutes, until almost set. (The center will not be completely firm.) When the cake has finished baking, remove it from the oven, loosen it from the edges of the pan by running a knife around the inside edge. Let the cheesecake cool for 30 minutes at room temperature. Both steps help prevent the top from cracking.

Refrigerate the cheesecake until cold. Unmold the cake by again running a knife around the outside edge of the pan and then releasing the latch on the springform.

To serve, cut the cheesecake with a hot dry knife. (Dip the knife in hot water and then dry it off.)

Crust

*

½ pound (2 sticks) cold sweet butter
½ cup sugar
1½ cups flour
½ cup cocoa powder
Pinch salt
A 9-inch springform pan

*

To make the crust:
Combine the butter and sugar in the bowl of an electric mixer.
Using the paddle attachment, mix on low speed for 15
seconds. Add the flour, cocoa, and salt and continue mixing
on low speed until the dough comes together. This will
take about 5 minutes.

Put the dough on a lightly floured board and roll it
into a 10-inch circle. Line the bottom and ½ inch up the
sides of the springform pan. Freeze the crust for at least
1 hour.

Bake the crust in a preheated 225 degree oven
for 25 minutes. Set aside to cool.

Chocolate Hazelnut Poundcake
with Espresso Cinnamon Cream

Here, an already superb cake is
beautifully enriched with a mound of espresso cinnamon cream.
Serves 10

Chocolate Hazelnut Poundcake:

¾ cup cocoa powder

1 cup flour

¼ teaspoon baking powder

½ teaspoon salt

6 ounces (1½ sticks) soft sweet
    butter

1½ cups sugar

1 teaspoon vanilla extract

3 large eggs

½ cup buttermilk

2 tablespoons water

4 ounces hazelnuts, toasted,
    skinned, and coarsely chopped

1 recipe Vanilla Custard Sauce
    (page 246)

A 9-inch bundt pan

Espresso Cinnamon Cream:

8 ounces mascarpone

3¼ cups heavy whipping cream

½ teaspoon vanilla extract

1 tablespoon espresso grounds

1 teaspoon ground cinnamon

2 tablespoons sugar

Pinch salt

Preheat the oven to 350 degrees.

Butter the bundt pan.

Sift together the cocoa powder, flour, baking powder, and salt. Set aside.

Put the butter and the sugar in the bowl of an electric mixer. With the paddle attachment, cream on medium high speed for 2 minutes, until light and fluffy. Continuing to mix, beat in the eggs, 1 at a time. Add the vanilla extract.

Combine the buttermilk and the water. Fold in the dry ingredients alternately with the buttermilk mixture. Stir in the chopped hazelnuts.

Spread the batter into the prepared pan and bake for about 30 minutes. A skewer inserted in the middle should come out clean.

Cool the cake and then invert to unmold it.

Serve with espresso cinnamon cream (see below) and vanilla custard sauce.

To make the espresso cinnamon cream: Combine all the ingredients in the bowl of an electric mixer. With the whisk attachment, whip the cream on high speed until it holds its shape. Refrigerate until ready to use.

Cornmeal Poundcake *with* Blackberries *and* Double Cream

*Cornmeal poundcake toasted for breakfast and served
with honey is divine, but toasted and served with blackberries
and rich cream, it is transcendental.*

Serves 8

2 ounces (½ stick) plus

   1 tablespoon soft sweet butter

1 cup brown sugar, firmly packed

½ cup sugar

5 large eggs

¾ cup sour cream

¾ teaspoon almond extract

½ teaspoon vanilla extract

Pinch salt

1¼ cups flour

1½ teaspoons baking powder

1 cup cornmeal

4 cups blackberries

1 recipe Double Cream (page 252)

A 9½- by 5½- by 3-inch loaf pan

Preheat the oven to 350 degrees.

Butter the loaf pan.

Combine the butter, brown sugar, and sugar in the bowl of an electric mixer. Using the paddle attachment, cream on medium high speed for 2 minutes, until light and fluffy.

Continuing to mix, add the eggs one at a time.

Stir in the sour cream and the almond and vanilla extracts on medium low speed, mixing well.

Sift together the salt, flour, and baking powder. On low speed, fold the dry ingredients and the cornmeal into the butter mixture. Pour the batter into the prepared pan.

Bake the poundcake for about 1 hour and 10 minutes, until a skewer inserted in the middle comes out clean.

Cool the cake and unmold it by running a knife around the inside edge and inverting the pan.

Preheat the broiler. Cut the poundcake into thick slices and toast it. Serve it immediately, topped with blackberries and double cream.

Orange Spice Cake
with Raspberries *and* Blackberries

Poundcake hardly needs embellishment,
but an already fulfilling cake is brought to new heights
when glazed and perfumed with fresh berries.
Serves 10

Poundcake:

½ pound (2 sticks) soft sweet butter

3 tablespoons finely ground dried
  bread crumbs

1½ cups sugar

3 large eggs

1 cup milk

2 tablespoons freshly squeezed
  lemon juice

Grated rind of 2 oranges

¾ teaspoon peeled and grated fresh
  ginger root

3 cups flour

½ teaspoon ground white pepper

¾ teaspoon ground cinnamon

1½ teaspoons ground cardamom

¾ teaspoon baking soda

¾ teaspoon baking powder

¾ teaspoon salt

A 10-inch bundt pan

Preheat the oven to 350 degrees.

Butter the bundt pan and line the pan with the bread crumbs.

Put the butter and the sugar in the bowl of an electric mixer. With the paddle attachment, cream on medium high speed for about 3 minutes, until light and fluffy. Continuing to mix, add the eggs 1 at a time.

In a small bowl, mix together the milk, lemon juice, orange zest, and ginger.

Sift together the flour, white pepper, cinnamon, cardamom, baking soda, baking powder, and salt. Add these dry ingredients alternately with the milk mixture to the creamed butter.

Bake the poundcake for about 40 minutes, until a skewer inserted in the middle comes out clean.

Let the cake cool for 15 minutes and then unmold it.

Glaze

*

½ cup sugar
¼ cup freshly squeezed orange juice
1½ teaspoons freshly squeezed lemon juice

*

3 cups raspberries
3 cups blackberries
1 recipe Chantilly Cream
(page 252)

*

Combine the sugar and the orange and lemon juices in
a small saucepot. Dissolve the sugar over low heat.
Brush the glaze on the cake. It will seem like a lot of glaze
but the cake will absorb all of it.
Cool the cake to room temperature before serving.

Serve with the raspberries, blackberries, and
chantilly cream.

Plum Cardamom Cake

One may not think of using cardamom (either yellow or green)
in the context of desserts, but its influence on plums will convert you forever.
Serves 8 to 10

Plum Syrup:

8 ounces (2 sticks) sweet butter

1 cup firmly packed brown sugar

8 to 10 plums, sliced ½ inch thick

A 9-inch round cake pan

Cake:

1½ cups cake flour

2 teaspoons baking powder

¾ teaspoon ground cardamom

¼ teaspoon salt

2 ounces (½ stick) soft sweet butter

1 cup sugar

½ cup plus 1 tablespoon milk

1 teaspoon vanilla extract

2 large eggs

1 recipe Vanilla Custard Sauce

(page 246)

To make the plum syrup:
Melt the butter in a small saucepot. Remove it from the stove and stir in the brown sugar. Pour the syrup into the bottom of the cake pan. Cover the syrup with the sliced plums. Set aside.

To make the cake:
Preheat the oven to 350 degrees.

Sift together the cake flour, baking powder, cardamom, and salt. Set aside.

Put the butter and sugar in the bowl of an electric mixer. With the paddle attachment, cream on medium high speed for 3 minutes, until light and fluffy.

Combine the milk and vanilla extract.

Alternately add the dry ingredients and milk mixture to the creamed butter in 3 additions. Beat on medium speed for 2 minutes, until smooth. Add the eggs, one at a time, and continue beating for another minute.

Pour the cake on top of the plums. Bake the cake at 350 degrees for about 55 minutes, until a skewer inserted in the middle comes out clean.

Remove the cake from the oven, and let it cool for 10 minutes. Run a knife around the inside edge of the pan and then invert the cake onto a plate.

Serve the cake warm or at room temperature with vanilla custard sauce.

Chocolate Silk

This silky, soft, luscious, chocolate-lover's dessert is incredibly rich.
Unlike a lot of "decadent" chocolate desserts, this stops just short of being excessive.
Serves 10 to 12

Crust:

3 ounces toasted and coarsely
    chopped walnuts

4 ounces toasted and coarsely
    chopped pecans

½ cup firmly packed brown sugar

Pinch ground cinnamon

4 ounces (1 stick) sweet butter,
    melted

A 9-inch springform pan

Mousse Cake:

20 ounces extrabittersweet chocolate

6 ounces (1½ sticks) soft sweet
    butter

¾ cup sugar

6 large eggs

¼ cup heavy whipping cream

½ teaspoon vanilla extract

To make the crust:
Combine the walnuts and pecans with the brown sugar and cinnamon in a stainless steel bowl. Stir in the melted butter. Press the nut mixture into the bottom of the springform pan.

Refrigerate the crust for ½ hour, until firm.

To make the mousse cake:
Melt the chocolate in the top half of a double boiler.

While the chocolate is melting, combine the butter and sugar in the bowl of an electric mixer. Using the paddle attachment, cream on medium speed until the mixture is light and fluffy.

Switch to the whisk attachment and add the eggs 2 at a time, mixing well after each addition. Scrape the sides of the bowl, increase to medium-high speed, and whip for 2 minutes, until the egg mixture increases slightly in volume.

Whisk the melted chocolate until it has cooled slightly. It should be warm but not hot.

Whisk the chocolate into the egg mixture on medium-low speed. Scrape the sides and bottom of the bowl and continue to mix until the chocolate is fully incorporated. Stir in the cream and vanilla extract.

Spread the mousse filling in the springform pan on top of the crust. Refrigerate the cake until firm, 6 hours to overnight.

Topping

*

1 cup heavy whipping cream
2 tablespoons sugar

*

To make the topping:
Put the cream and sugar in the bowl of an electric mixer.
With the whisk attachment, whip on high speed
until soft peaks form. Spread the whipped cream on top of
the cake. Unmold the cake from the pan by running
a hot dry knife around the inside edge of the pan and then
releasing the latch from the springform.
Slice the cake with a hot dry knife.
(Dip the knife in hot water and then dry it off.)

Torta Regina

*This flavorful cake is very light, so it can easily handle the addition of both ice cream
(Caramel or Hazelnut, pages 116 and 119) and the Orange Custard Sauce (page 246).
It can also be eaten plain in the afternoon with espresso or a glass of Vin Santo.*
Serves 8

5½ ounces hazelnuts, toasted and

skinned

5½ ounces bittersweet chocolate,

finely chopped

1 teaspoon lemon zest

2 teaspoons orange zest

6 large eggs, separated

½ cup sugar

A 9-inch round cake pan

Preheat the oven to 350 degrees.

Line the bottom of the cake pan with parchment paper.

Put the hazelnuts, chocolate, and lemon and orange zests in a food processor fitted with the metal blade. Finely grind the mixture using on-off pulses. Set aside.

Combine the egg yolks and ¼ cup of the sugar in the bowl of an electric mixer. With the whisk attachment, whip on high speed for about 3 minutes, until slightly increased in volume. Decrease the speed to low and stir in the ground nut mixture. The batter will be very stiff.

Put the egg whites in a separate bowl of an electric mixer. With the clean whisk attachment, whip on medium speed until frothy. Increase to high speed and whip the whites until soft peaks form. Continuing to whip, add the remaining ¼ cup sugar, and whip the whites until stiff.

Fold one-half of the egg whites into the batter. When they are almost completely incorporated, fold in the remaining egg whites. Pour the batter into the prepared pan.

Bake the cake for about 25 minutes, until a skewer inserted in the middle comes out clean.

Cool the cake and then unmold it.

Serve the cake with caramel or hazelnut ice cream and orange custard sauce.

Spiced Pecan Cake *with* Mascarpone Cream Cheese Frosting

One morning at Stars we discovered some leftover fabulous spiced pecans from a banquet menu the night before. We came up with this traditional layer cake to use them.

Serves 10 to 12

Spiced Pecan Cake:

4½ cups Candied Pecans

  (page 238)

8 ounces (2 sticks) soft sweet butter

2½ cups plus 2 tablespoons sugar

2¼ cups cake flour

2¼ cups all-purpose flour

3 tablespoons baking powder

1½ teaspoons salt

1½ cups milk

1 tablespoon vanilla extract

4 egg whites

Three 9-inch cake pans

To make the cake:
Preheat the oven to 325 degrees.

Line the bottoms of the cake pans with parchment paper.

Put 3 cups of the candied pecans in a food processor fitted with the metal blade and finely grind them. Reserve the remaining 1½ cups of pecans for decorating the top of the cake.

Put the butter and 2 cups of the sugar in the bowl of an electric mixer. Using the paddle attachment, cream on medium high speed until light and fluffy.

Sift together the cake flour, all-purpose flour, baking powder, and salt. Set aside.

Combine the milk and the vanilla. On low speed, alternately add the milk and the dry ingredients to the butter mixture. Fold in the ground candied pecans.

Put the egg whites in a clean bowl of the electric mixer. Using the whisk attachment, whip the whites on medium speed until frothy. Increase to high speed and whip the whites until soft peaks form. Continuing to mix, add the remaining ½ cup plus 2 tablespoons sugar. Whip until stiff.

Fold one-half of the egg whites into the pecan batter. When they are almost completely incorporated, fold in the remaining egg whites. The batter will be quite stiff. Spread it in the prepared pans.

Bake the cakes for about 40 minutes, until a skewer inserted in the middle comes out clean. Cool the cake layers and then unmold them. Frost the sides and top of the three cake layers with the mascarpone cream cheese frosting (see recipe opposite), making a 3-layer cake. Decorate the top with the reserved pecans.

Mascarpone Cream Cheese Frosting

*

Yield: enough for one 3-layer cake
¾ pound cream cheese
4 ounces (1 stick) soft sweet butter
1 cup sugar
1 teaspoon vanilla extract
1½ pounds mascarpone

*

To make the frosting:
Put the cream cheese, butter, sugar, and vanilla
in the bowl of an electric mixer. Using the paddle attachment,
beat on medium speed until smooth. Decrease to low
speed and add the mascarpone. Beat just until incorporated,
about 30 seconds. (Do not overbeat or the mascarpone
will separate.) Refrigerate until ready to use.

Butter Almond Cake *with* Strawberries *and* Caramel Cream

Born in the student kitchen of our now illustrious sous chef Hollyce, this dessert got her her job at Stars. Be sure to use almond paste without preservatives.

Serves 8 to 10

10 ounces almond paste

1¼ cups plus 1½ tablespoons sugar

8 ounces (2 sticks) soft sweet butter

Chopped zest of 2 oranges

6 large eggs

1 cup cake flour, sifted

½ teaspoon baking powder

Pinch salt

2 pints strawberries, hulled and
    quartered

1 recipe Caramel Cream (page 253)

A 10-inch bundt pan

Preheat the oven to 350 degrees.

Butter the bottom and sides of the bundt pan.

Put the almond paste in the bowl of an electric mixer. With the paddle attachment, beat on medium speed for about 2 minutes, until malleable. Slowly mix in the 1¼ cups of sugar. Beat in the butter and orange zest until creamy. Add the eggs 1 at a time. Beat the mixture until well combined and increased in volume.

Fold in the sifted cake flour, the baking powder, and the salt.

Spread the batter into the prepared pan. Bake the cake for 35 to 40 minutes until a skewer inserted in the middle comes out clean. Cool the cake and then unmold it.

To serve, slice the almond cake into wedges and top with caramel cream and sliced strawberries.

Drunken Chocolate Cake

This cake is an adaptation from Bjorn Olson, a good cook turned architect,
and a friend of Jeremiah's. It is aptly named because of the amount of rum in it.
Serves 8 to 10

Chocolate Cake:

6 ounces bittersweet chocolate,
   coarsely chopped

5 ounces (1¼ sticks) sweet butter

⅔ cup dark rum

4 large eggs, separated

1¼ cups sugar

1 cup flour

Pinch salt

1 recipe Chantilly Cream
   (page 252)

A 9-inch round cake pan

Bittersweet Chocolate Glaze:

1 cup heavy whipping cream

8 ounces bittersweet chocolate

To make the cake:
Preheat the oven to 350 degrees.

Line the bottom of the cake pan with parchment paper.

Melt the chocolate, butter, and rum in the top half of a double boiler. Set it aside to cool to lukewarm.

Combine the egg yolks and ½ cup plus 3 tablespoons of the sugar in the bowl of an electric mixer. With the whisk attachment, whip the egg mixture on high speed for 3 minutes, until thick. Decrease to medium-low speed and stir in the chocolate mixture. Stir in the flour and salt.

Put the egg whites in a separate bowl of an electric mixer. With the clean whisk attachment, whip them on medium speed until frothy. Increase the speed to high and whip until soft peaks form. Add the remaining sugar and continue beating until stiff. Fold one-third of the egg whites into the chocolate batter. When they are almost completely incorporated, gently fold in the remaining whites. Pour the batter into the prepared pan.

Bake the cake for 30 to 35 minutes, until a skewer inserted in the middle comes out clean.

When the cake is cool, unmold it and frost it with the bittersweet chocolate glaze.

To make the chocolate glaze:
Put the cream in a heavy-bottomed sauce-pot and bring it to a boil over high heat. Remove the cream from the heat and whisk in the chocolate until it is smooth.

Cool the glaze to room temperature and frost the sides and top of cake. Allow the cake to rest for at least 1 hour before cutting. Cut with a hot dry knife (dip the knife in hot water and then dry it off).

Serve the cake with chantilly cream.

Tuscan Cream Cake

*The Saturday before Easter, my husband's family and I go shopping in North Beach,
the Italian section of San Francisco. Moving from store to store, we buy focaccia, raviolis,
cold cuts, Italian cheeses, bread sticks, wines, espresso, and cookies. We take it all home,
spread it on the table and enjoy a huge feast. The meal ends with a thick slice of
Sacripantina from Stella Pastry Shop on Columbus Avenue. A sponge cake layered with
zabaglione cream, this cake is an adaptation of their version.*

Serves 10

1 recipe Zabaglione (page 245)

2 recipes Sponge Cake (page 236)

1½ cups heavy whipping cream

¼ cup sugar

1 cup chocolate shavings

¾ cup crushed amaretti cookies

A 9-inch springform pan

To assemble the cake:

Cut the sponge cakes into three 9-inch circles and then cut each circle in half horizontally, to make six 9-inch circles. You will need only 5 layers for this cake. (Freeze the extra cake pieces to use in trifles.)

Put a cake circle in the bottom of a 9-inch springform pan. Top the cake layer with 1¼ cups of zabaglione. Continue layering cake and zabaglione in this manner, ending with a layer of cake. You will have 5 layers of cake and 4 layers of zabaglione.

Refrigerate the cake for 1 to 2 hours to allow it to set.

Unmold the cake by running a hot dry knife around the edge of the pan and then releasing the latch on the springform.

Put the heavy cream and the sugar in the bowl of an electric mixer. With the whisk attachment, whip on high speed until soft peaks form. Frost the sides and top of the cake. Decorate the top with chocolate shavings and the sides with the crushed amaretti.

Gingerbread *with* Warm Apples *and* Cider Sabayon

Cutting the gingerbread in boxes and serving it with
warm apples and Cider Sabayon makes this an elegant dessert.
Serves 6

Gingerbread

1½ cups boiling water

1 cup molasses

1 teaspoon baking soda

4 ounces (1 stick) soft sweet butter

1 cup firmly packed light brown
  sugar

1 large egg

½ teaspoon salt

2 teaspoons ground ginger

1¼ teaspoons ground cinnamon

Pinch ground cloves

2½ cups flour

1 tablespoon baking powder

1 recipe Cider Sabayon (page 245)

A 9- by 13-inch pan

Warm apples:

7 medium-sized firm, juicy apples

2 tablespoons sweet butter

½ cup sugar

2 tablespoons calvados

2 tablespoons freshly squeezed
  lemon juice

Pinch salt

To make the gingerbread:
Preheat the oven to 350 degrees.

Butter the bottom and sides of the pan.

Bring the water to a boil in a small pot and remove it from the heat. Stir in the molasses and the baking soda. Set the molasses mixture aside to cool to lukewarm.

Combine the butter and sugar in the bowl of an electric mixer. With the paddle attachment, cream on medium-high speed for about 2 minutes, until light and fluffy. Continuing to mix, add the egg.

Sift together the salt, ginger, cinnamon, cloves, flour, and baking powder. Alternately fold the dry ingredients and the cooled molasses mixture into the butter and egg mixture on low speed. Pour the batter into the prepared pan.

Bake the gingerbread for 30 to 35 minutes, until a skewer inserted in the middle comes out clean. When it is cool, cut it into 2- by 3-inch rectangles. Remove some of the center of each piece with a small knife or melon baller.

To assemble:
Fill the box with warm apples (see below) and top with cider sabayon.

To make the apples:
Peel, core, and slice the apples ³⁄₁₆ inch thick. Melt the butter in a large sauté pan over medium heat. Add the remaining ingredients. Cook the apples, stirring occasionally, until they are soft but still retain their shape.

Grandmothers' Chocolate Cake

One-half of this cake comes from my grandmother, and the other half from my husband's
grandmother. I grew up eating the chocolate frosting and my husband grew up eating the cake.
Put the components together and all that's missing is a tall glass of milk.
Serves 10 to 12

Chocolate Cake:

1½ cups plus 1 tablespoon cocoa
powder

1¼ cups boiling water

1½ cups cake flour

1½ cups plus 2 tablespoons all-
purpose flour

1¼ teaspoons baking powder

1¼ teaspoons baking soda

5 ounces (1¼ sticks) soft sweet
butter

2¾ cups firmly packed brown sugar

3 large eggs

1¼ cups buttermilk

1¼ teaspoons vanilla extract

Three 9-inch round cake pans

To make the cake:
Preheat the oven to 350 degrees.

Butter the cake pans.

Whisk together the cocoa and the boiling water in a small bowl, making a smooth paste. Set aside to cool.

Sift together the cake flour, all-purpose flour, baking powder, and baking soda.

Put the butter and brown sugar in the bowl of an electric mixer. With the paddle attachment, cream them on medium-high speed for 2 minutes, until light and fluffy.

Add the eggs, 1 at a time, beating well after each addition.

Decrease to low speed, and stir in the dry ingredients alternately with the buttermilk and vanilla extract. Add the reserved cocoa paste. Divide the batter evenly among the 3 pans.

Bake the layers for about 25 minutes, until a skewer inserted in the middle comes out clean.

When the cakes are cool, unmold them by running a knife along the inside edge of each pan and inverting them.

Frost with bittersweet chocolate frosting (see recipe opposite), making a 3-layer cake.

Bittersweet Chocolate Frosting

★

4 ounces bittersweet chocolate
8 ounces unsweetened chocolate
8 ounces (2 sticks) sweet butter
3½ cups powdered sugar
Pinch salt
2 teaspoons vanilla extract
⅞ cup (1 cup minus 2 tablespoons) milk

★

To make the frosting:
Melt the chocolates and the butter over
a pot of simmering water. Let the mixture
cool to lukewarm.

Sift together the powdered sugar and salt
into a large bowl.

Combine the vanilla and the milk.
Whisk the milk into the powdered sugar. Add the
melted chocolate mixture and stir until smooth.

Chocolate Marble Boxes

*Always featured at Stars for special parties, these individual
cakes are real show-stoppers.*

Serves 6

12 Chocolate Meringue Shells

    (page 247)

1 recipe Caramel Cream

    (page 253)

12 ounces white chocolate,

    finely chopped

10 ounces bittersweet chocolate,

    coarsely chopped

1 cup white chocolate shavings

1 cup dark chocolate shavings

1 recipe Vanilla Custard Sauce

    (page 246)

A pastry bag with ½-inch tip

Parchment paper

Put 6 meringue shells on a tray. Put the caramel cream in a pastry bag fitted with a ½-inch tip. Pipe out ¼ cup of caramel cream onto each of the meringue shells. Top with a second meringue shell. Refrigerate the meringue shells until ready to wrap them.

Put the chopped chocolates into two separate bowls and melt them over pots of simmering water.

Measure the height of each of the meringue shells. They will be about 2 inches high. Cut 6 pieces of parchment paper long enough to just wrap around the individual cakes and tall enough to come ¼ to ½ inch above the top of each cake.

Lay the parchment strips on the work surface. Spread about 2 tablespoons of the melted white chocolate evenly over the piece of parchment paper with a flat knife or metal spatula. Drizzle about 1½ tablespoons of dark chocolate over the white chocolate and swirl the two chocolates together with the end of a zester or the tines of a fork. (As you swirl the two chocolates they will blend together and become dark-colored on the surface. The underside of the chocolate will be the show side and will have a marbleized pattern. You can peel back a corner of the parchment paper and see what the pattern looks like.) Swirl the two chocolates together until the pattern on the underside is nicely marbleized.

Let the marbleized chocolate paper set for 2 or 3 minutes, then carefully pick up the chocolate-swirled parchment paper and carefully wrap it around the layered meringue circles.

Continue to wrap the other boxes in the same manner.

Refrigerate the boxes for about 1 hour, until the chocolate hardens.

Carefully and slowly peel the parchment paper from the chocolate. Decorate the top of each box with white and dark chocolate shavings.

Refrigerate the boxes until ready to serve, and serve with vanilla custard sauce.

Orange Angelfood Cake *with* Caramelized Pears

An old favorite, gussied up and still wonderful.
Yield: one 10-inch cake

Orange Angelfood Cake :

1½ cups egg whites

1¼ teaspoons cream of tartar

1½ cups sugar

1 cup cake flour, sifted

Pinch salt

1 teaspoon vanilla extract

2½ tablespoons chopped orange zest

1 teaspoon freshly squeezed lemon
   juice

1 recipe Raspberry Sauce
   (page 251)

A 10-inch angelfood cake pan

Caramelized Pears:

8 ripe pears, peeled, cored, and
   sliced ⅓ inch thick

⅓ cup sugar

1½ tablespoons freshly squeezed
   lemon juice

2 tablespoons brandy

Pinch salt

Preheat the oven to 350 degrees.

Put the egg whites in the bowl of an electric mixer. Using the whisk attachment, whip them on medium speed until frothy. Add the cream of tartar. Increase to high speed and continue to mix, slowly pouring in the sugar. Continue whipping until the whites hold a stiff peak but still look moist.

Remove the bowl from the machine and fold in the flour, salt, vanilla extract, orange zest, and lemon juice.

Gently scoop the batter into the cake pan. Bake for about 30 minutes, until a skewer inserted in the middle comes out clean.

When the cake has finished baking, invert the pan and allow it to cool upside down. If your angelfood pan does not have legs for it to rest on when it is inverted, invert the inner tube of the pan onto a bottle. When the cake is completely cool, run a knife around the inside edge of the pan and then invert the pan.

To make the pears:
Combine the pears with the other ingredients in a 12-inch sauté pan. Cook over medium high heat for 10 to 15 minutes, until the sugar starts to caramelize lightly and the pears are soft but still retain their shape. As they begin to color, stir the pears gently to prevent them from burning.

Serve the cake with warm or at room temperature caramelized pears and raspberry sauce.

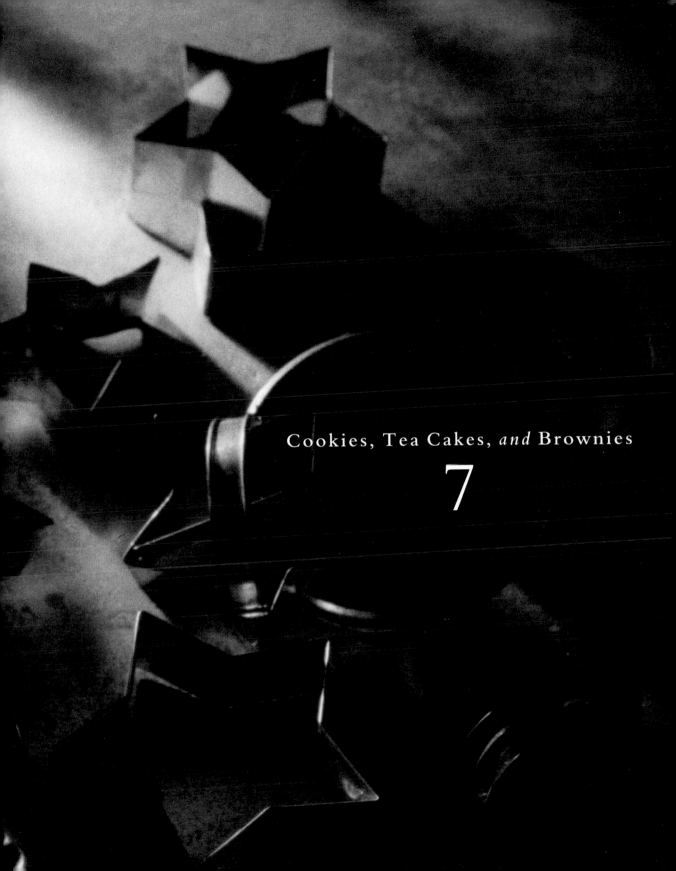

Cookies, Tea Cakes, *and* Brownies

7

*

Cookies should be simple and straightforward.

Unlike other desserts which have sauces and creams

to heighten their flavors, the cookies at Stars

stand on their own merits. They are like concentrated desserts;

they have as much flavor and give the same

level of satisfaction as a refined dessert.

I always have an assorted cookie plate on the menu

for our customers who want a little something sweet

but cannot decide exactly what they would like.

*

Black *and* White Brownies

Black and white brownies are very popular at StarMart,
where office workers often stop by for a mid-afternoon snack. The cream cheese
adds richness yet lightens the otherwise heavy chocolate texture.
Yield: one 9- by 13-inch pan

5 ounces bittersweet chocolate

2 ounces unsweetened chocolate

7 ounces (1¾ sticks) soft
  sweet butter

2 cups sugar

5 large eggs

¾ cup plus 1 tablespoon flour

Pinch salt

20 ounces cream cheese

1 teaspoon vanilla extract

Preheat the oven to 325 degrees.

Butter the sides and bottom of a 9- by 13-inch pan.

Melt the chocolates in a double boiler. Allow to cool slightly.

Combine the butter and 1¼ cups of the sugar in the bowl of an electric mixer. Using the paddle attachment, cream on medium speed until light and fluffy. Continuing to mix, add 3 of the eggs and beat well. Stir in the melted chocolate and mix until smooth. Decrease to low speed and stir in the flour and salt.

Spread the chocolate batter in the pan, reserving about 1 cup for later use.

Combine the cream cheese and the remaining ¾ cup of sugar in a clean bowl of an electric mixer. Using the paddle attachment, beat on medium speed until smooth. Add the remaining 2 eggs and the vanilla extract and again beat until smooth.

Spread the cream cheese mixture in an even layer over the chocolate batter. Scatter spoonfuls of the reserved chocolate batter over the cream cheese mixture. With a knife, swirl the chocolate batter into the cream cheese mixture, creating a marble pattern.

Bake the brownies for 50 to 55 minutes, until a skewer inserted in the middle comes out with a moist crumb. Cool for at least ½ hour before cutting.

Ginger Cookies

In the private dining room at Stars, we serve these cookies
hot out of the oven at the end of a meal. They are without a doubt
the favorite cookies of the Stars staff.
Yield: 3 dozen cookies

1 cup granulated sugar

½ cup firmly packed light brown
   sugar

8 ounces (2 sticks) soft sweet butter

1 large egg

⅓ cup molasses

2 teaspoons ground ginger

½ teaspoon ground allspice

1 teaspoon ground cinnamon

2 teaspoons baking soda

½ teaspoon salt

¼ teaspoon ground white pepper

2¼ cups flour

Preheat the oven to 325 degrees.

Put ½ cup of granulated sugar, the brown sugar, and the butter in the bowl of an electric mixer. With the paddle attachment, cream the butter on medium speed for 2 minutes, until the mixture is light and fluffy. Continuing to mix, beat in the egg and then the molasses. On low speed, add the dry ingredients and mix until incorporated. Refrigerate the dough for 30 minutes.

Roll the dough into ¾-inch balls and roll them in the remaining ½ cup of sugar. Line a baking sheet with parchment paper. Put the cookies 2 or 3 inches apart on the baking sheet. Flatten them slightly with 2 fingers.

Bake the cookies for about 12 minutes, until golden brown and set around the edges but still soft inside. Let them cool for 5 minutes and then remove them from the baking sheet.

Chocolate Chip Cookies

There are an infinite number of chocolate chip cookie recipes,
but this has to be among the best. Big and full of chips, these cookies are loyal to the Toll House
tradition, yet are not too cloyingly sweet.
Yield: 2½ dozen

8 ounces (2 sticks) soft sweet butter

1 cup firmly packed light brown
  sugar

1 cup firmly packed dark brown
  sugar

2 large eggs

1 tablespoon vanilla extract

2½ cups flour

1 teaspoon baking soda

1 teaspoon salt

2½ cups chocolate chips

Preheat the oven to 350 degrees.

Put the butter in the bowl of an electric mixer. Using the paddle attachment, cream the butter on medium speed for 2 minutes until light and fluffy. Continuing to mix, slowly add the brown sugars, and again beat until light and fluffy. Add the eggs 1 at a time, and then the vanilla, mixing until well incorporated. Fold in the dry ingredients and the chocolate chips.

Chill the dough for 30 minutes.

Form the dough into 1½-inch balls. Line a baking sheet with parchment paper and put the cookies 3 or 4 inches apart on the baking sheet. Chill the cookies for at least 1 hour before baking. (This prevents them from spreading while baking.)

Bake the cookies for about 15 minutes, until golden brown. Let them cool for 10 minutes and then remove them from the baking sheet.

Biscotti

This recipe was developed by Jules Vranian, one of the first pastry chefs at Stars.
Traditional Italian cookies, biscotti are great dipped in coffee or a glass of Beaumes de Venise.
Yield: 2½ dozen

2¾ cups flour

1⅔ cups sugar

½ teaspoon salt

1 teaspoon baking powder

1 teaspoon anise seeds

Chopped zest of 1 lemon

Chopped zest of 1 lime

Chopped zest of 1 orange

3 large eggs

3 large egg yolks

1 teaspoon vanilla extract

7 ounces whole almonds, skin on

Preheat the oven to 325 degrees.

Put the flour, sugar, salt, baking powder, anise seeds, and the chopped zest in the bowl of an electric mixer. Combine, using the paddle attachment on medium low speed. In a separate bowl with a whisk, lightly beat together the eggs, egg yolks, and vanilla extract. Continuing to mix, pour the egg mixture into the dry ingredients. When the eggs are almost completely incorporated, reduce the speed to low, add the almonds, and mix just until the dough comes together.

Roll the dough into 3 logs, each about 10 inches by 2 inches. Line a baking sheet with parchment paper. Place the logs on the baking sheet and bake for about 20 minutes, until light brown. Let the logs cool.

Decrease the oven temperature to 300 degrees. Cut the biscotti logs at a slight diagonal, ¾ inch thick. Return the cookies to the baking sheet, with a cut side up. Bake the biscotti for 15 minutes, until golden brown and dry.

Variation:
Dip one side of the cut and baked biscotti in melted chocolate. Put the biscotti, chocolate side down, on waxed or parchment paper and refrigerate until the chocolate is set, about half an hour.

Chinese Almond Cookies

These cookies, a recipe from Katherine, a cook at Restaurant 690,
are similar to ones found in Chinatowns everywhere.
They are a favorite at both Stars and at The Peak Cafe in Hong Kong.
Yield: 3 dozen

8 ounces (2 sticks) soft sweet butter

2 cups powdered sugar

1 tablespoon water

1 teaspoon baking powder

½ teaspoon baking soda

1 large egg

¾ teaspoon almond extract

2 cups flour

1 ounce sliced almonds, toasted

36 whole almonds for garnish

1 large egg, slightly beaten

Preheat the oven to 325 degrees.

Put the butter in the bowl of an electric mixer. Using the paddle attachment, cream the butter on medium speed until smooth. Continuing to mix, slowly add the sugar and beat until light and fluffy. Stir together the water, baking powder, and baking soda and add it to the butter mixture. Beat in 1 egg and the almond extract. Decrease to low speed and fold in the flour and sliced almonds.

Refrigerate the dough for about 1 hour until firm. Roll the dough into two 1-inch logs. Slice each log into ½-inch slices. Place the cookies several inches apart on a parch-ment-lined baking sheet. Press a whole almond into the middle of each cookie. Brush the cookies with the beaten egg.

Bake for about 10 minutes, until golden brown. Cool the cookies for 5 minutes and then remove them from the baking sheets.

Cinnamon Sugar Cookies

*Slightly underbaking these cookies will result in a soft, chewy texture,
while leaving them in the oven for the full amount of time will make them crisp.*
Yield: 2 dozen

4 ounces (1 stick) soft sweet butter

¾ cup plus 1½ tablespoons sugar

1 large egg

1⅓ cups flour

1 teaspoon cream of tartar

½ teaspoon baking soda

Pinch salt

1½ teaspoons ground cinnamon

Preheat the oven to 350 degrees.

Combine the butter and ¾ cup of the sugar in the bowl of an electric mixer. With the paddle attachment, cream the butter on medium speed until light and fluffy. Add the egg and beat until smooth. Stir together the flour, cream of tartar, baking soda, and salt. Fold the flour mixture into the butter mixture.

Mix together the remaining 1½ tablespoons sugar and the cinnamon. Form the dough into 1-inch balls and roll them in the sugar mixture. Line a baking sheet with parchment paper and put the cookies several inches apart on the pan.

Bake the cookies for 8 to 10 minutes, until golden brown. Allow them to cool for 5 to 10 minutes and then remove them from the baking sheet.

Macaroons

You can vary the taste of macaroons by the kind of honey you use.
California wild flower honey, French lavender honey, or an Australian blue gum honey
produce equally good but quite different results.
Yield: 3½ dozen

1 cup egg whites

2½ cups sugar

2 tablespoons honey

2 teaspoons vanilla extract

15 ounces shredded sweetened
   coconut

1¼ cups cake flour, sifted

8 ounces bittersweet chocolate

Whisk together the egg whites, sugar, honey, and vanilla extract in a large stainless steel mixing bowl.

Put the bowl over a pot of simmering water. Whisking occasionally, heat the mixture to the temperature of warm bath water.

Remove the bowl from the heat and fold in the coconut and the flour.

Refrigerate the dough until firm and mold it into 1-inch balls.

Preheat the oven to 300 degrees.

Line a baking sheet with parchment paper and put the cookies, several inches apart, on the pan. Bake them for 15 to 20 minutes, until golden brown. Cool the macaroons for about 10 minutes and then remove them from the pan.

Melt the chocolate over a double boiler. With a knife, spread a thin layer of chocolate on the bottom of each macaroon. Line another sheet pan with parchment paper and place the cookies, chocolate side down, on the pan.

Refrigerate the macaroons for about 1 hour, until the chocolate hardens.

Russian Tea Cakes

*Many Eastern European countries have versions of this cookie,
but this is the favorite of Yugoslavia-born Denise Hale, a great friend
of Jeremiah's, who commissions them for her ranch weekends. You can substitute
hazelnuts or walnuts for the pecans or use a mixture of all three.*
Yield: 3 dozen

6 ounces pecans, toasted

6 tablespoons granulated sugar

8 ounces (2 sticks) soft sweet butter

½ teaspoon vanilla extract

2 cups flour

½ teaspoon salt

¼ cup powdered sugar

Preheat the oven to 300 degrees.

Put the pecans and 2 tablespoons of the granulated sugar in a food processor fitted with the metal blade. Finely grind the pecans and set them aside.

Put the butter and the remaining 4 tablespoons of granulated sugar in the bowl of an electric mixer. Using the paddle attachment, cream the butter on medium speed for 2 or 3 minutes, until light and fluffy. Add the vanilla extract. Combine the flour and salt and stir into the butter mixture. Add the reserved nuts.

Form the dough into ¾-inch balls. Line a baking sheet with parchment paper and put the cookies on the pan, 2 inches apart.

Bake the tea cakes for about 20 minutes, until light brown. While they are still warm, sprinkle them with the powdered sugar.

Brown Butter Madeleines

A traditional tea cake of Proustian fame, madeleines are good with a cup of hot tea or an espresso.
They are miraculous when made with imported French butter, with its added richness.
(See page 258 for mail order sources.) The use of brown butter gives them an added twist.
Yield: 3 dozen 3-inch cookies

6 ounces (1½ sticks) sweet butter

2 tablespoons soft sweet butter

¾ cup plus 3 tablespoons flour

4 large eggs

Pinch salt

⅔ cup sugar

1 teaspoon chopped lemon zest

1 teaspoon vanilla extract

Powdered sugar (for dusting
   the cookies)

3 dozen 3-inch madeleine molds

Preheat the oven to 350 degrees. Melt the 6 ounces of butter in a small pot. Heat the butter over medium heat until it is brown and gives off a nutty aroma. Strain and cool the butter to room temperature.

Butter the madeleine molds with the 2 tablespoons soft butter. Dust the molds with the 3 tablespoons flour. Invert the pans and tap out any excess flour.

Put the eggs with the salt in the bowl of an electric mixer. Whip on high speed until thick, about 3 minutes. Continuing to mix on high speed, slowly add the sugar in a steady stream and whip for 2 minutes, until the mixture is thick and ribbony. Decrease to low speed and add the lemon zest and vanilla extract.

By hand, fold one-third of the flour into the batter, followed by one-third of the melted butter. Continue folding the remaining flour and butter, one-half at a time, into the batter. Spoon the batter into the prepared molds, filling them two-thirds full.

Bake the madeleines for about 10 minutes, until golden brown. They should spring back when lightly touched. Remove them from the oven and unmold immediately by hitting the edge of the pan on the counter. When cool, dust with the powdered sugar.

Stareos

These are "gourmet" Oreos, a rich chocolate shortbread "sandwich"
with a mascarpone filling. They are best when eaten the day they are made.
Yield: 1½ dozen cookies

Cookies:

8 ounces cold sweet butter

½ cup sugar

1½ cups flour

Pinch salt

½ cup cocoa powder, sifted

The filling:

1 cup mascarpone

1 tablespoon sugar

¼ teaspoon vanilla extract

To make the chocolate shortbread:
Combine the butter and sugar in the bowl of an electric mixer. Mix on low speed for 15 seconds, using the paddle attachment. Add the flour, salt, and cocoa powder and continue mixing on low speed for 3 to 5 minutes, until the dough comes together. It will look dry just before it comes together.

Put the dough on a lightly floured board and roll it out ¼ inch thick. With a 2-inch star cutter, cut out the cookies. Chill them for 1 hour in the freezer. Line a baking sheet with parchment paper and place the cookies so they are not touching on the pan.

Preheat the oven to 250 degrees.

Bake the shortbread for about 1 hour, until firm.

To make the filling:
Combine the mascarpone, sugar, and vanilla extract in a small bowl.

To assemble:
Spread about 1 tablespoon of the mascarpone cream filling on 18 of the cookies. Put the remaining uncoated cookies on top of the creamed cookies, making a "sandwich."

Chocolate Meringue Cookies

These cookies have the best of everything:
They are crunchy on the outside and gooey in the middle.
Yield: 3 dozen

3 egg whites

1 cup sugar

6 ounces chocolate chips

2 tablespoons cocoa powder, sifted

½ teaspoon vanilla extract

Preheat the oven to 275 degrees.

Put the egg whites in the bowl of an electric mixer. Whip them on medium high speed until frothy. Increase to high speed and slowly add the sugar. Continue whipping until stiff. Remove the bowl from the machine, and by hand fold in the remaining ingredients. The batter should not be completely mixed; it should have some brown and white streaks.

Line a baking sheet with parchment paper. Drop 2 tablespoons of batter for each cookie several inches apart onto the baking sheet.

Bake the cookies for 35 minutes. They should be dry on the outside but still soft inside. Cool for 5 to 10 minutes before removing them from the pan.

When cool, store in an airtight container.

Shortbread Cookies

We have been baking shortbread at Stars since we first opened. Over the years,
adaptations have been created, but we can never decide which one we like the best!
For a Meals on Wheels gala at New York's Rockefeller Center, I made 3,500 shortbread
cookies, packed them very carefully, and flew them to New York. You can freeze the rolled-
out, unbaked shortbread dough and place it in the oven straight from the freezer.
Yield: 2 dozen

8 ounces (2 sticks) cold sweet butter

½ cup sugar

2 cups flour

Pinch salt

Preheat the oven to 250 degrees.

Combine the butter and sugar in the bowl of an electric mixer. Using the paddle attachment, mix on low speed for 15 seconds. Add the flour and salt and continue mixing on low speed for 3 to 5 minutes, until the dough comes together. It will look dry just before it comes together.

Put the dough on a lightly floured board and roll it out ¼ inch thick. With a 3-inch star cutter or other desired shape, cut out the cookies. Chill them for 1 hour in the freezer or refrigerator.

Line a baking sheet with parchment paper and place the cookies, so they are not touching, on the pan. Bake the shortbread for about 45 minutes, until firm. They should remain white in color.

Variations:
Hazelnut Shortbread:
Add ½ cup finely ground toasted and skinned hazelnuts to the master shortbread recipe.
Espresso Shortbread:
Use the master shortbread recipe but decrease the flour by ¼ cup and add ¼ cup of espresso grounds.
Orange Shortbread:
Add 3 tablespoons chopped orange zest to the master shortbread recipe.
Cinnamon Shortbread:
Add 1 teaspoon of ground cinnamon to the master shortbread recipe.

Lemon Squares

Another popular snack with the workers in the federal and state offices
near Stars. A line often forms waiting for these to cool so that they can be sliced.
We always seem to sell out, no matter how many we make.
Yield: One 9- by 13-inch pan

Crust:

1½ cups flour

½ cup powdered sugar

6 ounces (1½ sticks) cold sweet
    butter

Filling:

6 large eggs

3 cups sugar

1 cup plus 2 tablespoons freshly
    squeezed lemon juice

½ cup flour

Powdered sugar for dusting

To make the crust:
Preheat the oven to 325 degrees.

Combine the flour and the powdered sugar
in the bowl of an electric mixer. Using the
paddle attachment, add the butter and mix
on low speed until mixture is the size of
small peas. Press the crust into the bottom
of a 9- by 13-inch pan.

Bake the crust for about 20 to 25 minutes,
until golden brown.

To make the filling:
Decrease the oven temperature to
300 degrees.

Whisk together the eggs and sugar in a
large bowl until smooth. Stir in the lemon
juice and then the flour. Pour the lemon
filling on top of the crust.

Bake the lemon bars for about 40 minutes,
until the lemon filling is set.

Allow them to cool for ½ hour, slice
into squares, and dust with the ¼ cup
powdered sugar.

Date Bars

Be sure to use fresh dates for these moist, juicy bars,
as the dates' sweetness and flavor are what make these so good.
Yield: one 9- by 13-inch pan

3¼ cups fresh dates, pitted

3 cups flour

3 ounces (¾ stick) soft sweet butter

3 cups light brown sugar, firmly
   packed

6 large eggs

⅓ cup water

1 tablespoon vanilla extract

1 tablespoon baking powder

4½ teaspoons ground cinnamon

¼ teaspoon salt

¼ teaspoon ground cloves

4 ounces pecans, toasted and
   coarsely chopped

Powdered sugar for dusting

Preheat the oven to 325 degrees.

Butter a 9- by 13-inch pan.

Put the dates and the flour in a food processor fitted with the metal blade. Process using on-off pulses, until the dates are in pieces about ⅓ of an inch in size. Set aside.

Put the butter and the brown sugar in the bowl of an electric mixer. Using the paddle attachment, cream on medium speed for about 2 minutes, until light. Slowly add the eggs and then the water and vanilla extract. Mix until smooth.

Decrease to low speed and add the baking powder, cinnamon, salt, and cloves. Mix in the ground dates and the pecans.

Spread the batter in the prepared pan. Bake the date bars for 25 minutes, until a skewer inserted in the middle comes out clean.

Cool the date bars to room temperature and dust them with the powdered sugar. Cut and serve.

Butterscotch Coconut Bars

Traditional blonde brownies, which combine chocolate chips in a brown sugar batter,
are jazzed up here with the addition of coconut and pecans.
Yield: One 9- by 13-inch pan

12 ounces (3 sticks) soft butter

3 cups firmly packed light brown
  sugar

3 large eggs

1 teaspoon vanilla extract

4 cups flour

½ teaspoon salt

¾ teaspoon baking soda

1½ cups chocolate chips

4 ounces pecans, toasted and
  chopped

½ cup shredded coconut

Preheat the oven to 350 degrees.

Butter the sides and bottom of a 9- by
13-inch pan.

Combine the butter and brown sugar in the
bowl of an electric mixer. Using the paddle
attachment, beat on medium speed for
1 minute. Continuing to mix, add the eggs
and vanilla and beat until light and fluffy.
On low speed, fold in the flour, salt, baking soda, chocolate chips, pecans, and coconut. Spread the batter in the prepared pan.

Bake the bars for about 25 minutes, until a
skewer inserted in the middle comes out
clean. Cool for at least ½ hour before cutting.

Breakfast

8

*

While not strictly desserts, the breakfast pastries

included in this chapter are an integral part of Stars Café

and StarMart. Breakfast should not be the forgotten meal,

where one is resigned to bland and mundane food,

eaten just because it is easy and convenient.

One is much more apt to get out of bed in the morning

(and to get others up as well)

if there are warm apple turnovers, pear ginger muffins,

or buttery cinnamon rolls waiting to be devoured.

*

Cinnamon Rolls

Everyone loves cinnamon rolls. Here's Stars' variation.
Yield: 12 rolls

Dough:

2¾ cups all-purpose flour

2 tablespoons sugar

½ teaspoon salt

1 tablespoon dry yeast

3 tablespoons lukewarm milk

3 large eggs

6 ounces (1½ sticks) very soft sweet
   butter

A 9- by 13-inch pan

Cinnamon Butter:

8 ounces (2 sticks) soft sweet butter

2¼ teaspoons ground cinnamon

¾ cup brown sugar

3 ounces pecans, toasted and
   coarsely ground

Combine the flour, sugar, and salt in a bowl and set it aside.

In a small bowl, dissolve the yeast in the milk and let it sit for 15 minutes. Place the eggs in the bowl of an electric mixer. Using the paddle attachment, mix in the yeast-milk mixture. Add the dry ingredients on low speed and mix until incorporated.

Increase to medium low speed and mix in the butter. Continue to mix until the butter is completely incorporated, scraping the sides of the bowl as necessary. Place the dough on a lightly floured board and knead by hand for about 5 minutes, until it is smooth and satiny. Place the dough in a bowl, cover it with a towel, and let it rise for 1 to 2 hours, until doubled.

While the dough is rising, prepare butter:

To make the cinnamon butter:
Put the butter, cinnamon, and brown sugar in the bowl of an electric mixer. Using the paddle attachment, beat on medium speed until creamy.

On a lightly floured board roll out the dough into a rectangle 18 by 11 inches. Spread the cinnamon butter evenly over the dough. Sprinkle the ground pecans over the cinnamon butter. From the long end, roll up the dough. Pinch the ends of the roll to the sides to seal it. Cut the log into 12 even pieces. Turn the rolls cut side up, and shape them with your hands into rounds.

Place the rolls with a cut side up in the lightly buttered pan. Cover them with plastic wrap and let them rise for several hours until doubled. (They can be allowed to rise overnight in the refrigerator. The morning that they are to be baked, transfer them from the refrigerator to the preheated oven.)

Preheat the oven to 350 degrees. Bake the rolls for 35 minutes, until they are golden brown.

While the cinnamon rolls are baking, prepare the royal icing:

Royal Icing:

*

1 cup powdered sugar
1½ tablespoons water

For the royal icing:
Whisk together the powdered sugar and water in a small bowl.

When the rolls have finished baking, remove them
from the oven, let them sit for 5 minutes, and then remove them
from the pan. When they have cooled slightly, drizzle
the royal icing over them.

Variation: Sticky Buns

*

Use the preceding recipe but put the following sauce into the
bottom of the pan before you put in the cinnamon rolls and omit
the royal icing.

1 cup Karo syrup
1½ cups cold Caramel Sauce (page 238)
1½ cups pecan halves, toasted

Whisk together the Karo syrup, caramel sauce, and pecans in a
bowl. Pour the sauce into the bottom of the pan.

Peach Butter

Everyone is familiar with apple butter. But once you make
your own peach or plum butter for toast or waffles,
or serve it warm over ice cream, you will rarely go back to apple.
Yield: about 4 cups

5 pounds peaches (about 12 large)

1½ cups sugar

2 teaspoons freshly squeezed
   lemon juice

Pinch salt

Preheat the oven to 300 degrees.

Halve and pit the peaches. Purée them through a food mill. There should be about 2 quarts of peach purée. Place the purée in a heavy-bottomed nonaluminum pot and stir in the sugar.

Bake the purée for 2½ hours, stirring every half-hour. Transfer the peach butter to a smaller clean pot. (As it reduces the edges of the pot get very dark.) Continue baking for another 2 to 2½ hours, until the peach purée is reduced to about 4 cups.

Let the butter cool and serve on toast and muffins. This keeps indefinitely in the refrigerator.

Variation:
For plum butter, substitute 5 pounds (about 30) plums for the peaches.

Cinnamon Toast

Gerald Nachman, a San Francisco newspaper columnist, challenged Jeremiah
to come up with a recipe for cinnamon toast the way the old hotels used to make it.
This Stars Café version is the only way to make cinnamon toast.
The broiled sugar and cinnamon make a crust that melts in your mouth.
Serves 4

2 teaspoons cinnamon

¼ cup sugar

8 pieces Brioche (page 244),
*   or other bread suitable for*
*   toasting*

2 tablespoons soft sweet butter

Preheat the broiler.

Mix together the cinnamon and sugar in a small bowl.

Toast the bread on both sides until golden brown. Brush the butter on one side of the toast and sprinkle the cinnamon sugar over the butter.

Return the toast to the broiler and broil until the cinnamon sugar bubbles.

Serve immediately.

Walnut Roll
(see following page)

Walnut Roll

The Yugoslavian name for this recipe is potica (pronounced po-teet-za),
and it has been passed down through my husband's family. The slices are delicious
served either plain or toasted.
Serves 8 to 10

Dough:

3½ cups flour

¼ cup sugar

1 teaspoon salt

2½ teaspoons dry yeast

½ cup water

½ cup milk

1 large egg

4 ounces (1 stick) soft sweet butter

Combine 1 cup of the flour, the sugar, salt, and yeast in the bowl of an electric mixer fitted with the paddle attachment.

Heat the water, milk, and butter until warm, about 120 degrees. Gradually pour the milk mixture into the dry ingredients and beat for 2 minutes on medium speed.

Add the egg and ½ cup of flour and continue to beat the mixture on medium high speed for 2 minutes. Reduce the speed to low, add the remaining 2 cups of flour, and mix until combined.

Put the dough on a lightly floured board and knead by hand for about 10 minutes, until it is smooth and satiny.

Put the dough in a large buttered bowl and cover it with a towel. Let it rise in a warm place for about 1½ hours, until doubled.

While the dough is rising, prepare the walnut filling:

Walnut Filling

*

10 ounces toasted walnuts
4 ounces (1 stick) soft sweet butter
½ cup brown sugar
2 large eggs
½ teaspoon vanilla extract
1 teaspoon ground cinnamon

*

To make the walnut filling:
Put the walnuts in a food processor, finely grind them,
and set aside.

By hand or in a mixer, cream the butter
and the brown sugar until smooth. Stir in one egg,
vanilla extract, and cinnamon. Add the ground walnuts
and mix until incorporated. Set aside.

*

To make the roll:
Place the risen dough on a lightly floured board and roll it
into a 20- by 15-inch rectangle.

Spread the walnut filling evenly over the dough. From the long end,
roll up the dough, pinching the ends to the sides to seal it.
Pull the dough to a length of 25 inches and twist
the roll into a snail shape. Place it on a buttered or
parchment-lined baking sheet.

Let the dough rise for about 1½ hours, until doubled.

*

Preheat the oven to 325 degrees. Lightly beat the remaining egg
and brush it on the dough. Bake the walnut roll for 40 to 45
minutes, until it is a dark golden brown color.

Let the walnut roll cool for 10 to 15 minutes and then slice it.

Banana Pecan Bread

*The great advantage of this bread is that it improves with a day or so of aging. It is
even better toasted or warmed and then spread with butter or sour cream.
Yield: one 9½- by 5½- by 3-inch loaf pan*

8 ounces (2 sticks) soft sweet butter

1½ cups firmly packed light brown
   sugar

4 large eggs

1¼ cups mashed bananas
   (about 3 bananas)

2½ cups flour

½ teaspoon salt

1½ teaspoons baking powder

6 ounces coarsely chopped pecans

Preheat the oven to 350 degrees.

Butter the sides and bottom of the loaf pan.

Put the butter and sugar in the bowl of an
electric mixer. Using the paddle attachment,
beat on medium speed until light and creamy.
Add the eggs 2 at a time, mixing well after
each addition. Stir in the bananas, mixing
until incorporated. Reduce to low speed and
add the dry ingredients and the nuts.

Spread the batter into the prepared pan and
bake the bread for about 45 minutes, until a
skewer inserted in the middle comes out
clean. Let it sit in the pan for 30 minutes
and then turn it out.

Peach Streusel Coffee Cake

This recipe is an adaptation of the coffee cake recipe from my seventh grade
home economics class. I am sure Mrs. Hallahan would approve!
Serves 8 to 10

Streusel:

¾ cup firmly packed brown sugar

2 tablespoons ground cinnamon

6 tablespoons (¾ stick) sweet

  butter, melted

6 tablespoons flour

Cake:

4 ounces (1 stick) sweet butter

1½ cups sugar

2 large eggs

1 cup milk

3 cups all-purpose flour

1 tablespoon plus 1 teaspoon

  baking powder

1 teaspoon salt

2 cups ½-inch-thick slices peeled

  peaches (about 4 medium peaches)

A 9- by 13-inch baking pan

To make the streusel:
Stir together all of the streusel ingredients in a mixing bowl and set aside.

To make the cake:
Preheat the oven to 350 degrees.

Butter the baking pan.

Put the butter and sugar in the bowl of an electric mixer. Using the paddle attachment, cream the mixture on medium speed until light and fluffy. Continue mixing, adding the eggs and then the milk.

Fold in the dry ingredients.

Spread half of the batter into the prepared pan and top with half of the streusel and the peaches. Spread the remaining batter over the peaches and top with the remaining streusel.

Bake the coffee cake for about 30 minutes, until a skewer inserted in the middle comes out clean. Cool for 10 to 15 minutes and then serve.

Apple Cream Cheese Turnovers

The dough and apples can be prepared a day ahead, refrigerated overnight, and easily assembled the morning they are to be eaten. Let the dough sit at room temperature for 15 to 30 minutes before rolling.

Yield: 8

8 ounces cream cheese

8 ounces (2 sticks) soft sweet butter

2 tablespoons sugar

¼ cup heavy whipping cream

Pinch salt

2½ cups flour

1 tablespoon sugar

1 teaspoon ground cinnamon

1 large egg, lightly beaten

Apples:

8 medium-sized firm, juicy apples

¾ cup sugar

2 ounces (½ stick) sweet butter

¼ teaspoon salt

2 tablespoons freshly squeezed
    lemon juice

Put the cream cheese, butter, the 2 tablespoons sugar, and cream in the bowl of an electric mixer. Using the paddle attachment, beat on medium speed until well blended. Add the salt and flour and mix until incorporated. Refrigerate the dough for 1 hour.

To make the apple filling:
Peel, core, and slice the apples ³⁄₁₆ inch thick. Place them in a large sauté pan with all of the other ingredients.

Cook the apples over medium heat until they are soft but still retain their shape. Cool before using.

Preheat the oven to 350 degrees.

Put the dough on a lightly floured board and roll it out ⅛ inch thick. Cut the dough into eight circles, each 7 inches in diameter.

Mix together the 1 tablespoon sugar and the cinnamon in a small bowl. Set aside.

To assemble:
Put ⅓ cup of the apple mixture on one side of each tart. Brush the outside ¼ inch of the circle with the beaten egg and fold the dough in half, forming a half circle. Press the sides together and fold the edge over to seal the turnover. Cut three air slits, each about ¼ inch long, in the top of the turnover. Brush with the beaten egg and sprinkle with the cinnamon sugar.

Bake the turnovers for 20 minutes, until golden brown. Serve warm.

Pohanas

Mark Franz, the executive chef at Stars, has shared
this recipe from his grandmother. Children and adults alike love them.
They are fun to make as they puff up when cooked.
Yield: about 3 dozen

2 large eggs

1¼ teaspoons unflavored oil

6 tablespoons lukewarm water

2¼ teaspoons freshly squeezed
   lemon juice

1½ teaspoons vanilla extract

¼ cup sugar

½ teaspoon salt

2½ teaspoons baking powder

2½ cups flour

2 cups oil for frying

Lightly whisk together the eggs, unflavored oil, water, lemon juice, and vanilla.

Combine the dry ingredients in the bowl of an electric mixer, using the paddle attachment. Pour in the egg mixture, mixing until well combined.

Change to the dough hook and knead the dough for about 3 minutes. Place the dough on a lightly floured board and finish kneading by hand until it is smooth and satiny. Place it in a greased bowl, cover it with a dish towel, and let it rest for ½ hour.

Put half the dough on a lightly floured board and roll it out ⅛ inch thick. Repeat with the second half of dough. Let the dough rest for ½ hour and then roll it out 1/16 inch thick. Cut the dough into ¾-inch strips.

Heat the 2 cups of oil in a large skillet or sauté pan. Drop a few strips of dough into the oil and cook them for a minute or two until golden brown. Place on paper towels and dust with granulated sugar. Continue to cook the remaining strips. Eat the pohanas while they are still warm.

Hollyce's Oatmeal Scones

*Developed for the opening of Stars Cafe, Hollyce's scones have taken
the neighborhood by storm. Eat them with jam and Double Cream (page 252).*
Yield: 10 scones

3 cups plus 2 tablespoons flour

½ cup plus 2 tablespoons sugar

1¼ teaspoons salt

1¼ teaspoons baking soda

2½ teaspoons baking powder

10 ounces (2½ sticks) cold sweet
    butter

2 cups oats

1 cup currants

2 tablespoons finely chopped
    orange zest

¾ cup buttermilk

Preheat the oven to 350 degrees.

Combine the flour, sugar, salt, baking soda, baking powder, and butter in the bowl of an electric mixer. Using the paddle attachment, mix at low speed until the butter is the size of small peas. Add the oats, currants, and chopped orange zest. Continue to mix, slowly pouring in the buttermilk, just until the dough comes together.

Put the dough on a lightly floured board and roll it out into a ¾-inch-thick circle. Cut the dough into 10 circles, each 3½ inches in diameter. Put the scones on a parchment-lined baking sheet and bake them for approximately 20 minutes, until golden brown.

Sour Cherry Muffins

Dried sour cherries, most commonly from Michigan, have a wonderful tangy flavor.
They are great in breakfast muffins, as they do not make them too sweet.
Yield: 12 medium muffins

1⅔ cups dried sour cherries

6 ounces (1½ sticks) sweet butter

1 cup firmly packed light brown
  sugar

3 large eggs

2½ tablespoons milk

1¼ teaspoons vanilla extract

2 cups flour

1¼ teaspoons baking powder

¾ teaspoon salt

½ teaspoon baking soda

Preheat the oven to 350 degrees.

Paperline the muffin tins or butter them.

Cover the sour cherries with hot water and soak them for 15 minutes. Drain the cherries and set them aside.

Put the butter and brown sugar in the bowl of an electric mixer. Using the paddle attachment, beat on medium speed until light and fluffy. Continue mixing and add the eggs, milk, and vanilla extract. Fold in the dry ingredients and the reserved cherries.

Spoon the batter into the prepared muffin tins.

Bake the muffins for about 30 minutes, until a skewer inserted in the middle comes out clean. Let the muffins sit for 5 minutes and then turn them out.

Pear Ginger Muffins

*A delicious morning eye-opener, even better
when the ginger is fresh crop Hawaiian and the pears have
a tablespoon of pear liqueur added to them.*
Yield: 18 medium muffins

7 ounces (1¾ sticks) sweet butter

¾ cup firmly packed light brown
    sugar

6 tablespoons granulated sugar

2 large eggs

¼ cup milk

1 teaspoon vanilla extract

2½ cups flour

1½ teaspoons baking powder

½ teaspoon baking soda

Pinch salt

1 tablespoon peeled and grated fresh
    ginger root

2 cups peeled, cored, and coarsely
    chopped pears

Preheat the oven to 325 degrees.

Paperline the muffin tins or butter them.

Put the butter and the sugars in the bowl of an electric mixer. Using the paddle attachment, beat on medium speed until light and creamy. Add the eggs and then the milk and vanilla.

Combine the dry ingredients and fold them into the butter mixture. Stir in the ginger and the pears. Do not overmix the batter or the muffins will be tough.

Spoon the batter into the prepared pans and bake the muffins for about 30 minutes, until a skewer inserted in the middle comes out clean. Let the muffins sit in the pan for 5 minutes and then turn them out.

Corn Blueberry Muffins

These muffins are best served just a few hours old, split in half,
toasted, and drizzled with honey.
Yield: 6 large

1 cup yellow cornmeal

1 cup flour

¼ cup sugar

2 teaspoons baking powder

1 teaspoon baking soda

½ teaspoon salt

¼ cup milk

2 large eggs

4 tablespoons (½ stick) sweet
   butter, melted

1 cup sour cream

2 cups blueberries

Preheat the oven to 350 degrees.

Paperline the muffin pans or butter them.

In a large bowl, combine the dry ingredients and set aside.

Whisk together the milk, eggs, melted butter, and sour cream in a separate bowl. Stir the egg-milk mixture into the dry ingredients. When the two mixtures are almost completely combined, add the blueberries. Do not overmix the batter or the muffins will be tough.

Put the batter into the prepared muffin tins. Bake the muffins for about 30 minutes, until a skewer inserted in the middle comes out clean. Let the muffins sit for 5 minutes and then turn them out.

Blackberry Sour Cream Muffins

These muffins are very easy to make,
and with wild blackberries and a large dollop of maple butter
(maple syrup whisked into butter), they are divine.
Yield: 12 medium muffins

1 cup milk

½ cup sour cream

2 eggs

3½ cups flour

1 cup sugar

1½ tablespoons baking powder

½ teaspoon salt

6 ounces (1½ sticks) cold
    sweet butter

2 cups blackberries

¼ cup firmly packed light brown
    sugar

Preheat the oven to 350 degrees.

Paperline the muffin tins or butter them.

Whisk together the milk, sour cream, and eggs in a mixing bowl and set aside. Combine the dry ingredients in the bowl of an electric mixer, using the paddle attachment on low speed. Add the butter and mix until the butter is the size of small peas. Pour the sour cream mixture into the butter and flour mixture and mix just until the dough comes together.

Gently fold the blackberries into the batter.

Spoon the batter into the prepared tins. Sprinkle the brown sugar on top.

Bake the muffins for about 25 minutes, until a skewer inserted in the middle comes out clean.

Let the muffins sit for 5 minutes and then turn them out.

Breton Galette

For Jeremiah, this rich but very simple thin cake with its buttery
lemon flavor is one of the most satisfying all-purpose snacks.
It is delicious and tastes best not hot but warm. If possible use French butter
when baking the galette. (See page 258 for mail order sources.)
Serves 6

2½ teaspoons dry yeast

⅓ cup warm water

7 ounces (1¾ sticks) soft sweet
    butter

¾ cup sugar

1 large egg

1½ cups flour

¼ teaspoon salt

1 teaspoon finely chopped
    lemon zest

1 ounce (¼ stick) cold sweet butter

Preheat the oven to 350 degrees.

Dissolve the yeast in the water and let rest in a warm place for 10 minutes.

Put the soft butter and ½ cup of the sugar into the bowl of an electric mixer. Using the paddle attachment, mix on medium speed until smooth. Add the yeast and the egg, mixing well. On low speed, stir in the dry ingredients and the lemon zest and mix just until combined. The dough will be very sticky.

Sprinkle 2 tablespoons of sugar in the middle of a sheet pan. Place the dough on top of the sugar and sprinkle 1 tablespoon of sugar over the dough. Gently roll the dough out into a 10-inch circle. If the dough sticks to the rolling pin, sprinkle the remaining tablespoon of sugar on top of the dough and continue to roll it out. Cut the 1 ounce of cold butter into small pea-size pieces and place them on top of the galette.

Bake the galette for about 15 to 20 minutes, until golden brown.

Slice the galette into wedges and serve it warm.

Blueberry Brioche Tartlets

I have always thought blueberries, unless wild, really need a slight cooking
to bring out their best flavor. Here, combined with buttery brioche,
they are a perfect start to a weekend breakfast. Make the brioche the day before.
Yield: 8 tarts

6 cups blueberries

½ teaspoon freshly squeezed
   lemon juice

¼ cup plus 3 tablespoons sugar

½ recipe unbaked Brioche
   (page 244)

1 cup Crème Fraîche (page 253)

Eight 4½-inch tart shells with
   removable bottoms

Preheat the oven to 350 degrees.

Put the blueberries, lemon juice, and ¼ cup of the sugar in a saucepot. Cook over medium-low heat, stirring occasionally, for about 10 minutes, until the berries begin to give off some juice. Cool to room temperature.

On a lightly floured board, roll out the brioche ¼ inch thick and cut into eight 5-inch circles. Line the tart shells with the brioche. Fill the tart shells with the blueberries. Sprinkle the remaining sugar on top.

Bake the brioche tarts for about 20 minutes, until golden brown.

Serve them warm with the crème fraîche.

Basic Recipes

9

*

The recipes in this chapter are used throughout the book.

They are building blocks for all of Stars' desserts.

If possible, keep some of these basics on hand in the freezer

or refrigerator to create a last-minute dessert

for unexpected company, or for your own cravings.

Recipes for mascarpone and crème fraîche are included because

they are not always available throughout the country.

*

Sponge Cake

This is a very versatile cake recipe. When using sponge cake for trifles, try to make it a day ahead, because cake must be slightly stale in order to stay firm in the trifle. This cake freezes well. Note the variation for chocolate sponge cake.

1¼ cups flour
2½ teaspoons baking powder
Pinch salt
5 large eggs, separated
1¼ cups sugar
5 tablespoons boiling water
1 teaspoon vanilla extract
An 11½- by 17½-inch jelly roll
    pan, or a sheet pan with 1-inch sides

Preheat the oven to 350 degrees.

Line the bottom of a jelly roll pan with parchment paper.

Sift together the flour, baking powder, and salt. Set aside.

Put the egg yolks and sugar in the bowl of an electric mixer. Using the whisk attachment, whip on high speed until thick and pale yellow. Reduce to medium speed and slowly add the water and the vanilla. Scrape the sides and bottom of the bowl. Return to high speed and continue whipping for about 5 minutes, until mixture is again thick and ribbony.

Fold the dry ingredients into the egg-sugar mixture.

Put the egg whites in a separate bowl of an electric mixer. With the clean whisk attachment, whip on high speed until soft peaks form. Fold half of the whipped whites into the batter and then fold in the remaining whites. Spread the batter evenly into the pan.

Bake the cake for about 15 minutes, until it is golden brown and springs back when lightly touched.

Variation:

Chocolate Sponge Cake: Use the preceding recipe but decrease the flour to 1 cup and add ½ cup of sifted cocoa powder to the other dry ingredients.

Lemon Curd

Here is a tangy lemon curd recipe. Lemon curd is best used the day it is made. After that, it picks up a metallic flavor that you can taste on the roof of your mouth.

Yield: 2 cups

9 large egg yolks
3 large eggs
1 cup sugar
1 cup freshly squeezed lemon juice

Put the egg yolks, eggs, and sugar in a stainless steel bowl. Whisk them together and then stir in the lemon juice.

Put the bowl over a pot of simmering water and stir continually with a rubber spatula. When the curd starts to thicken, switch to a whisk. Cook the curd until thick. This will take about 5 minutes.

Strain the curd into a glass or plastic container and cover the surface directly with plastic wrap. This prevents a skin from forming.

Refrigerate the curd for several hours until cold. Use as directed.

Chocolate Sauce

We love the flavor of pure chocolate, as do millions of other people. We added as little cream as possible to this James Beard recipe to make it a truly chocolate chocolate sauce.

Yield: 5 cups

21 ounces bittersweet chocolate
3 cups heavy whipping cream

Coarsely chop the chocolate.

Pour the cream into a heavy-bottomed saucepot and scald it. Remove the pot from the stove and add the chocolate.

Cover the mixture and let it sit for 5 minutes. Stir the chocolate cream until smooth. Serve the sauce warm or refrigerate for later use.

This will keep for several weeks in the refrigerator. To reheat, warm the sauce over a double boiler.

Caramel Sauce

I always like to keep some caramel sauce on hand in the refrigerator. This recipe of James Beard's can be served warm over ice cream or quickly added to chantilly cream. Take care when you pour in the cream as the combination of hot and cold ingredients causes the mixture to bubble up.

Yield: 4 cups

3 cups sugar
1 cup water
2 cups heavy whipping cream

Combine the sugar and water in a heavy-bottomed saucepan. Dissolve the sugar in the water over low heat. Increase the heat to high and cook until the caramel is a golden amber color.

Remove the caramel from the heat and slowly whisk in the cream, a few tablespoons at a time. Be very careful, as the mixture will bubble as you add the cream.

Serve the sauce warm or refrigerate for later use.

This will keep for several weeks in the refrigerator. To reheat, warm over a double boiler.

Candied Pecans

These nuts are wonderful eaten plain, over ice cream, or in cakes.

Yield: 4½ cups

½ cup light brown sugar
3 tablespoons ground cinnamon
1 large egg white
2 tablespoons vanilla extract
14 ounces pecan halves

Preheat the oven to 300 degrees.

Combine the brown sugar and cinnamon in a stainless steel bowl and set aside.

Whisk the egg white in a separate bowl until frothy. Stir in the vanilla extract, the pecans, and then the reserved brown sugar mixture.

Spread the pecans evenly on a baking sheet and bake them for 30 minutes until they are dry.

Pastry Cream

Be sure always to cook pastry cream over medium low heat so that it doesn't become overcooked or grainy. Note the variations for other flavored pastry creams.

Yield: 3 cups

8 large egg yolks
½ cup sugar
Pinch salt
3 tablespoons cornstarch
2½ cups milk
One 4-inch piece vanilla bean
¼ cup heavy whipping cream
2 tablespoons sweet butter

Place the egg yolks, sugar, and salt in a mixing bowl and whisk until well blended. Stir in the cornstarch.

Put the milk and vanilla bean in a heavy-bottomed nonreactive pot. Scald the milk and then by hand whisk it slowly into the egg and sugar mixture, removing the vanilla bean.

Transfer the milk–egg mixture back to the pot and cook it over medium low heat, stirring constantly, for 3 to 5 minutes, until thick. Remove the pot from the heat and stir in the cream and butter. Strain, and place plastic wrap directly on the surface of the pastry cream to prevent a skin from forming.

Refrigerate the pastry cream for an hour or two until cold.

Pastry cream will keep for several days in the refrigerator.

Pastry Cream Variations:
Cinnamon Pastry Cream: Add one cinnamon stick and 1 teaspoon ground cinnamon to the milk before scalding.

Brown Sugar Pastry Cream: Substitute ½ cup firmly packed brown sugar for the granulated sugar.

Espresso Pastry Cream: Whisk 5 tablespoons of liquid espresso into the hot pastry cream before straining.

Ginger Pastry Cream: Add a 2-inch piece of fresh ginger root, roughly chopped, to the milk before scalding.

Stars' Sweet Pastry Dough

The trick to good pastry shell is not to add too much water (which will make the dough tough) and not to overwork the dough. Following these two rules will allow you to produce flaky, buttery pie and tart shells. Extra dough can be frozen, either in batches or rolled out in shells. Wrap the dough well and it will last for a week or two in the freezer. Simply thaw the dough and roll it out as desired. Always use tart forms with removable bottoms.

Enough dough for one of the following: One 9-inch tart and lattice, or one 10-inch pie and top, or six 4-inch tarts

2 tablespoons sugar
3 cups flour
¼ teaspoon salt
12 ounces (3 sticks) cold sweet butter
3 tablespoons (approximately) ice cold water

Combine the sugar, flour, and salt in the bowl of an electric mixer.

Using the paddle attachment, cut in the butter on low speed until it is the size of small peas.

Slowly pour in just enough water so that the dough just comes together. It should look rough in the bowl but hold together if you squeeze it in your hand. Too much water will make the tart dough tough.

Refrigerate tart and pie shells for 30 minutes before baking.

Dough rolling information:
Roll out pie shells and top shells ¼ inch thick.
Roll out tart shells ⅛ inch thick.
To make lattice, roll out the dough ⅛ inch thick and cut into ½-inch-wide strips.

To prebake a pie or tart shell:
Line the pie or tart shell with parchment paper and fill with uncooked rice or dried beans. Bake in a preheated 350-degree oven for about 15 minutes, until the edges of the shell are golden brown. Remove the paper and weights. Decrease the temperature to 325 degrees and continue baking the tart shell for about 15 minutes, until the bottom of the shell is golden brown.

To partially bake a pie or tart shell:

Bake the tart or pie shell with the parchment paper and the weights until the edges are golden brown, as described above. Remove the parchment paper and weights and bake for 5 minutes more.

If your tart shell cracks on the bottom, make a thick paste out of a little flour and water and seal the crack. Place the tart back in the oven for a few minutes to dry the "glue."

Pumpkin Purée

Making your own pumpkin purée is very simple, and the results are much superior to canned pumpkin. Use small sugar pumpkins, which have the sweetest, most flavorful flesh.

Yield: 2½ cups

2½ pounds sugar pumpkins
¼ cup water

Preheat the oven to 325 degrees.

Cut the pumpkins into sixths. Put the pumpkin pieces and the water in a roasting pan and cover the pan with aluminum foil.

Bake the pumpkin for about 1 hour and 10 minutes. The pumpkin should be soft.

Discard the seeds of the pumpkin and scoop the flesh out from the skin. Purée the flesh through a food mill or in a food processor.

Use as directed. Extra pumpkin purée can be frozen.

Crêpes

*Crêpes are quick and easy to make. They freeze won-
derfully when stacked between pieces of wax paper and
well wrapped in plastic wrap. Crêpes are ideal to have
on hand for a fast dessert: some fresh fruit juice, a knob
of butter, and sugar (powdered, superfine, or brown) and
you have a simple, satisfying dessert.*

Yield: 16 *crêpes*

2 large eggs
½ cup water
½ cup plus 2 tablespoons milk
1 cup flour
Pinch salt
1 ounce (¼ stick) melted sweet butter

Put the eggs, water, and ½ cup of the milk in a
stainless steel bowl. Whisk them together and then
add the flour and salt. Stir in the butter.

Refrigerate the batter for at least ½ hour to
overnight, and then strain it.

To make the crêpes:
Heat a 6-inch nonstick or seasoned crêpe pan over
medium heat. Pour 2 tablespoons of the batter into the
pan and quickly rotate the pan, spreading a thin layer
of batter over the entire bottom. Cook the crêpe for
a couple of minutes until golden brown. Invert the
crêpe with the edge of a knife or your fingers.
Cook the other side for about 30 seconds. Invert
the crêpe from the pan.

Proceed to make the rest of the crêpes in the same
manner. You can stack them as you make them.

If your first few crêpes are too thick, thin the
batter out with the extra milk.

Chocolate Crêpes

Chocolate crêpes have a great bittersweet chocolate flavor. They freeze as well as regular crêpes.

Yield: 16 *crêpes*

2 large eggs
¼ cup sugar
1 cup milk
½ cup flour
1 tablespoon cocoa powder
Pinch salt
1 tablespoon sweet butter, melted
1 tablespoon vanilla extract

Put the eggs, sugar, and milk in a stainless steel bowl. Whisk them together and then add the flour, cocoa powder, and salt. Stir in the butter and vanilla.

Refrigerate the batter at least 1 hour to overnight, and then strain it.

To make the crêpes:

Heat a 6-inch nonstick or seasoned crêpe pan over medium heat. Pour 2 tablespoons of the batter in the pan and quickly rotate the pan, spreading a thin layer of batter over the entire bottom. Cook the crêpe for a couple of minutes and then invert it with the edge of a knife or your fingers. Cook the other side for about 30 seconds. Invert the crêpe from the pan.

Proceed to make the rest of the crêpes in the same manner. You can stack them as you make them.

Brioche

A delicious bread to have on hand in and out of the freezer. It is great by itself for breakfast toasted with cinnamon; buttered and soaked with wild Tasmanian honey; or made into desserts like the summer pudding or pear charlotte.

Yield: 2 loaves, each 9½- by 5½- by 2

1 teaspoon dry yeast
½ cup warm water
3 tablespoons sugar
6 large eggs
5 cups all-purpose flour
1¾ teaspoons salt
11 ounces (2¾ sticks) soft sweet butter,
*   cut into 1-inch pieces*

Combine the yeast and water in the bowl of an electric mixer. Stir in the sugar and let stand for 10 minutes.

Using the paddle attachment on medium low speed, stir in the eggs. Add the flour and salt, mixing until the flour is almost completely incorporated.

Change the dough hook and slowly add the butter on medium low speed. When all of the butter has been added, increase to medium speed and knead the dough for about 5 minutes, until the butter is completely incorporated.

Put the dough in a bowl, cover it, and let it rise in a warm spot for about 2 hours, until doubled. (The dough can rise overnight in the refrigerator.)

Press the dough into 2 greased loaf pans and let it rise in a warm spot for about 2 hours until doubled.

Preheat the oven to 350 degrees.

Bake the bread for about 30 minutes. When the brioche is done it will be a dark brown color and when tapped on the bottom of the loaf, it should make a hollow sound. Remove it from the pans and place it on wire racks to cool.

Champagne Sabayon

Sabayon is a Stars staple. We always have several flavors around to be used on a moment's notice. It is imperative that the sabayon be whisked over ice until it is completely cold. It can be made a day ahead. Note the variations for other flavors of sabayon.

Yield: 5 cups

8 large egg yolks
½ cup sugar
Pinch salt
¾ cup Champagne
1 cup heavy whipping cream

Combine the egg yolks, sugar, and salt in a large stainless steel bowl. Whisk in the Champagne.

Fill a large bowl one quarter full of ice water and set aside. Place the first bowl over a pot of boiling water and whisk the egg mixture vigorously for about 5 minutes, until it is thick and tripled in volume. The sabayon should mound slightly when dropped from the whisk. Immediately put the bowl over the ice bath and whisk until cold.

Pour the cream into the bowl of an electric mixer. With the whisk attachment, whip on high speed until soft peaks form. Fold the cream into the sabayon.

Refrigerate until ready to use.

Sabayon Variations:
Cider Sabayon: Substitute ½ cup plus 2 tablespoons apple juice and 2 tablespoons calvados for the Champagne.

Grand Marnier Sabayon: Substitute ¼ cup Grand Marnier and ½ cup freshly squeezed orange juice for the Champagne.

Tangerine Sabayon: Substitute ½ cup freshly squeezed tangerine juice (about 6 tangerines) and ¼ cup light rum for the Champagne.

Basque Sabayon: Substitute 6 tablespoons Armagnac, 1 tablespoon orange flower water, 3 tablespoons dark rum, and 2 tablespoons anisette for the Champagne.

Zabaglione: Substitute ¾ cup marsala and ¼ cup sherry for the Champagne. Fold in 1½ cups heavy whipping cream (instead of 1 cup) to the cooled sabayon.

Vanilla Custard Sauce

Custard sauce (or crème anglaise) is for me where desserts start and end. It can be superb by itself (remember that, when frozen, it is ice cream) and there is hardly a fruit, cake, pudding, or cobbler-type dessert that is not enhanced, enriched, and graced by this delicious preparation.
Note the variations for other flavors of custard sauces.

Yield: 3½ cups

10 large egg yolks
3 tablespoons sugar
Pinch salt
3¼ cups milk
1 teaspoon vanilla extract,
*   or a 1-inch piece of vanilla bean*

Whisk together the egg yolks, sugar, and salt in a stainless steel mixing bowl until creamy. Set aside.

Put the milk and the vanilla extract or vanilla bean in a heavy-bottomed saucepot. Scald the milk, and slowly whisk it into the egg mixture.

Put the bowl over a pot of simmering water and cook the custard, stirring constantly with a wooden spoon, for about 5 minutes, until it begins to thicken. It should coat the back of the wooden spoon. Do not let it boil.

Cool the custard sauce over an ice bath. Strain and refrigerate until ready to use. Custard sauce will keep for 2 days in the refrigerator.

Custard Sauce Variations:

Coffee Custard Sauce: Add 3 tablespoons of ground dark roast coffee or espresso to the milk before scalding.

Orange Custard Sauce: Add the peel of 1 orange to the milk before scalding.

Chocolate Custard Sauce: Whisk ½ cup of warm chocolate sauce into the cooled and strained custard sauce.

Cinnamon Custard Sauce: Add ½ teaspoon cinnamon and 1 stick of cinnamon to the milk before scalding.

Rum Custard Sauce: Add 1 tablespoon of dark rum to the cooled and strained custard sauce.

Framboise Custard Sauce: Add 1½ tablespoons of framboise liqueur to the cooled and strained custard sauce.

Cognac Custard Sauce: Add 1½ tablespoons of Cognac to the cooled and strained custard sauce.

Chocolate Meringue Shells

Chocolate meringue shells can be used for a variety of desserts. The cocoa powder gives them more flavor than traditional plain meringues.

Yield: 18 shells

⅓ cup sugar
1 cup plus 2 tablespoons powdered sugar, sifted
7 tablespoons cocoa powder, sifted
7 large egg whites
¾ cup plus 3 tablespoons sugar

Preheat the oven to 225 degrees. Sift together the ⅓ cup sugar, the powdered sugar, and the cocoa powder. Set aside.

Line 2 sheet pans with parchment paper. With a pencil, draw eighteen 3-inch circles on the parchment paper. Place a ¼-inch plain round tip in a pastry bag.

Put the egg whites in the bowl of an electric mixer. Using the whisk attachment, whip on medium speed until frothy. Increase to high speed and gradually add the 3 tablespoons sugar, whipping until soft peaks form. Continuing to whip, slowly add the ¾ cup sugar, and whip until the whites are stiff and glossy and the sugar is dissolved.

Fold in the cocoa powder mixture.

"Glue" the corners of the parchment paper to the baking pans with small dabs of butter. Starting from the inside of the penciled circles, pipe the batter in a circular motion, making a solid coil. Continue to make the remaining meringues.

Bake until the meringues are dry and come easily off the paper, several hours to overnight.

Store in an airtight container until ready to assemble.

Puff Pastry

*Don't be alarmed at the thought of making your own
puff pastry—it just requires a little concentration. It
may take you a few tries to master the techniques, but be
patient and you will be able to produce flaky, light puff
pastry in no time. The actual working time is not long,
but seems that way because you have to allow time for
the dough to rest. Well-wrapped puff pastry will keep
for a week in the freezer. If possible, use French butter
to make puff pastry. (See page 258 for mail order
sources.)*

*Yield: ten 5- by 5-inch pieces ⅛ inch thick or twenty
    4- by 5-inch pieces 1/16 inch thick*

*2 cups plus about ½ cup flour
½ teaspoon salt
1 pound cold sweet butter
½ cup ice cold water*

Combine 2 cups flour and salt on the work surface.

Cut the butter into ¼-inch cubes. Toss the butter
with the flour and salt so that all the cubes are coated
with flour. Shape this mixture into a mound, leaving
a well in the center.

Pour the water into the well. With your fingertips, as though you were tossing a salad, work the
water in so that a rough dough begins to form. It
will look like torn and knotted rags. Gently press
the dough together so that all the dry flour is
absorbed. Form this into a rectangle approximately
6 inches by 8 inches and 1¼ inches thick. Wrap the
dough in plastic wrap and chill for 1 hour in the
refrigerator.

After this resting period, roll the dough on a
lightly floured board into a rectangle 7 inches by
16 inches, approximately ½ inch thick. (If you
notice the butter breaking through the flour, let the
dough sit out for 5 minutes at room temperature
before attempting to roll it.) With the short end of
the dough closest to you, fold the dough as you
would a letter; bring the top down two-thirds of
the way and fold the bottom over the top. This is a
single turn.

Give the dough a quarter turn so that the open seam is on your right and the closed seam on your left.

Repeat the folding and rolling process, giving the dough another single turn. Refrigerate the dough for 1 hour.

Give the dough 2 more single turns, rolling and folding, and making sure to give it a quarter turn between turns, and let it rest for another hour.

Again give the dough 2 single turns, folding and rolling, and allow it to rest in the refrigerator from 1 hour to overnight before rolling to desired thickness.

Tips for rolling the puff pastry:
Put the puff pastry on a floured surface. Sprinkle flour on top and roll to the thickness specified in recipe. Keep the sides of the puff pastry straight and even as you roll. Occasionally sprinkle flour underneath and on top to prevent the pastry from sticking.

Brush off excess flour. Cut the puff pastry by pressing the knife down with a rocking motion to make a clean cut. Do not drag the knife through the pastry. Freeze puff pastry pieces until ready to use.

To create the traditional mille-feuille (1,000 layers) for napoleons:
Pierce holes with the tines of a fork all over the puff pastry. This is called *docking* and prevents the dough from rising. Place an inverted wire mesh cooling rack over the puff pastry when baking to further prevent it from rising.

Simple Syrup

It's a good idea always to have simple syrup on hand. It will keep for weeks in the refrigerator. It is an excellent sweetener for ice tea or coffee, because you don't have to wait for the sugar to dissolve.

Yield: 3½ cups

2½ cups sugar
2 cups water

Mix the sugar and water in a small pot. Bring to a boil. Boil for 1 minute.

Cool the syrup, cover, and store it indefinitely in the refrigerator.

Praline

When making praline, you can use one type of nuts or a combination, which we prefer.

Yield: 2 cups

2 ounces toasted pecans
1 ounce sliced toasted almonds
2 ounces toasted and skinned
   hazelnuts
1 cup sugar
¼ cup water

Butter a baking sheet and set it aside.

Coarsely chop the nuts.

Combine the sugar and water in a heavy-bottomed saucepot. Over low heat, dissolve the sugar in the water. Increase to high heat and cook the sugar until it is a golden amber color.

Stir the nuts into the caramel and then pour the mixture onto the buttered baking sheet. Be careful, as the caramel is very hot. Allow the praline to cool and harden.

Tap the baking sheet on a counter or table to coarsely break up the praline. Place the praline in a food processor fitted with the metal blade and finely grind it, using on-off pulses.

Praline will last for about a week in a cool dry place.

Blueberry Sauce

This is wonderful over ice cream or served with cakes, puddings, and fruit trifles.

Yield: 2 cups

4 cups blueberries
¼ cup Simple Syrup (page 250)
1 teaspoon freshly squeezed lemon juice
Pinch salt

Put the blueberries in a heavy-bottomed saucepot. Add the simple syrup, lemon juice, and salt.

Cook the blueberries over medium heat until they begin to give off some of their juice.

Purée half of the blueberries in a food processor and then strain the purée through a medium-holed strainer. Stir the purée back into the blueberries.

Serve warm or at room temperature.

Berry Sauce

Use strawberries, raspberries, or blackberries for this recipe. The amount of sugar you need will depend on the sweetness of the berries.

Yield: 1 cup

1 pint strawberries (hulled),
raspberries, or blackberries
Approximately 2 tablespoons sugar
½ teaspoon freshly squeezed lemon juice
Pinch salt

Purée the berries through a food mill with a medium strainer or in a food processor fitted with the steel blade.

Strain the purée through a medium-holed sieve to eliminate any remaining seeds.

Stir in sugar, lemon juice, and salt. Taste the purée and adjust for sweetness.

Refrigerate until ready to use.

Chantilly Cream

Chantilly cream should be velvety in texture and just hold its shape. It will have the best flavor and texture when whipped by hand. If you overwhip it, try folding in some unwhipped cream. If possible, avoid using ultra-pasteurized cream, as it does not whip as well or hold its shape when whipped. Do not use powdered sugar to sweeten chantilly cream, as the cornstarch in the sugar gives it a chalky taste.

Yield: 4½ cups

*2¼ cups heavy whipping cream
    (not ultrapasteurized)
1 teaspoon vanilla extract
1½ tablespoons sugar
Small pinch salt*

Put all the ingredients in a large stainless steel bowl. Whisk the cream just until it holds its shape.

Refrigerate the cream until ready to use. Chantilly cream should be used within an hour after it is made. If you wait longer to use it, you may need to rewhip it slightly.

Double Cream

It is a shame that Devonshire cream, available in England, is so hard to find in the United States. We created double cream as a substitute.

Yield: 5 cups

*8 ounces mascarpone
2¼ cups heavy whipping cream
    (not ultrapasteurized)
½ teaspoon vanilla extract
2 tablespoons sugar
Small pinch salt*

Put all the ingredients in a large stainless steel bowl. Whisk the cream until it holds its shape.

Refrigerate the cream until ready to use. Double cream should be used within an hour after it is made. If you wait longer to use it, you may need to rewhip it slightly.

Crème Fraîche

Crème fraîche has a more tangy taste and is lighter than sour cream. If it is unavailable in your area, here is a recipe to make your own. This recipe is from Sadie Kendall of Kendall Farms in Atascadero, California. She makes crème fraîche commercially and has been supplying it to Stars since we opened. For pictures of her cheeses and farm, see Jeremiah's New American Classics.

Yield: 6 cups

6 cups heavy cream (not ultrapasteurized)
1 cup sour cream

Whisk together the heavy cream and the sour cream in a stainless steel or glass bowl. Cover the bowl with cheesecloth.

Let the cream sit at room temperature (around 68 degrees) until it thickens. This will take from 12 to 24 hours. Stir the crème fraîche until smooth and refrigerate it.

The crème fraîche will stay fresh for several weeks. As it ages it will give off some watery liquid. Either stir it back into the crème fraîche or spoon it off and discard it.

Caramel Cream

Superbly simple. Be sure to make enough, however, as everyone always wants another spoonful.

Yield: 3½ cups

4 ounces mascarpone
1½ cups heavy whipping cream
½ cup cold Caramel Sauce (page 238)
Pinch salt

Put all of the ingredients in a large stainless steel bowl. Whisk the cream just until it holds its shape.

Refrigerate the cream until ready to use. It should be used within an hour after it is made. If you wait longer to use it, you may need to rewhip it slightly.

Mascarpone

If you cannot find mascarpone in your area, here is a recipe to make your own. It does not have quite the creamy consistency of store-bought mascarpone, but it is a good substitute. Tartaric acid is a granular substance often used in wine-making.

Yield: 2 cups

4 cups heavy whipping cream
¼ teaspoon tartaric acid
*   (page 258 for mail order sources)*

Line a mesh strainer with a dish cloth folded over to make a double thickness. Rest the strainer over a bowl, making sure that the strainer does not touch the bottom of the bowl. Set aside.

Heat the cream in a double boiler over medium high heat. When the cream reaches 180 degrees, add the tartaric acid and stir it for 30 seconds.

Remove the cream from the stove and continue to stir for another 2 minutes.

Pour the cream into the lined strainer and refrigerate. When it is cold, cover it with plastic wrap. Let the cream sit in the refrigerator for 12 to 18 hours. It will become very thick and firm. The mascarpone will keep for a week in the refrigerator.

Appendix: Cooking Notes

Ingredients:

Chocolate

I prefer bittersweet chocolate to semisweet or milk chocolate, as it has a richer and deeper flavor. At Stars we use Cacao Barry, Callebaut, Ghirardelli, Guittard, and Valrhona chocolates. Lindt chocolate, widely available on the retail level, is also an excellent brand. Different desserts call for different types of chocolate. Extrabittersweet chocolate is a must for the chocolate silk, while bittersweet chocolate is good for chocolate sauce and most chocolate cakes. Use cocoa powder *made by dutch process, a method that reduces its acidity and gives it a smoother taste. Be sure to use white chocolate made with cocoa butter and not vegetable oils. Do not use chocolate candy bars in baking. Store chocolate well wrapped in foil in a cool, dark place. Dark chocolate will keep for at least 1 year under these conditions. White chocolate is more perishable and should be used within 6 months.*

To melt chocolate:

Coarsely chop the chocolate and place it in a stainless steel bowl over a pot of simmering water. Do not let the water touch the bottom of the bowl. Stir occasionally until the chocolate is melted and smooth. White chocolate is very susceptible to heat. Chop white chocolate finely so that it melts more evenly, and make sure to stir it often while it is melting.

To make chocolate shavings:

Lay a large piece of chocolate on a work surface. Place a towel against the end of the chocolate closest to you and push it against your hip. (The towel prevents the chocolate from getting all over you.) Hold a sharp knife, with one hand on each end, lengthwise across the chocolate and scrape the knife toward you over the chocolate. Alternatively, you can use a vegetable peeler on a smaller piece of chocolate. Three ounces of chocolate will produce about 2½ cups of shavings.

Dairy Products

Butter

Sweet butter *does not contain salt, and should be used in baking because it gives you control of the salt in recipes and has a purer taste. The shelf life of sweet butter is shorter than that of salted butter, so be sure to freeze it if you are not going to use it soon after you buy it. Some grocery stores sell sweet butter in the frozen food section. Always store butter well wrapped in the refrigerator, as it picks up odors easily.*

To clarify butter:

Place the butter in a double boiler and melt it slowly over medium low heat. Let the butter sit for 10 to 15 minutes and then skim the foam off the top. Spoon the remaining clear yellow liquid (the clarified butter) into a separate container, leaving behind the milk solids on the bottom.

Cream and milk

We always use whole milk *in baking. When we refer to cream in the recipes we use* heavy cream, *which is also called heavy whipping cream or manufacturing cream. Avoid ultrapasteurized cream, which has added preservatives that give it a chemical taste. It also does not whip as nicely as heavy cream. You can substitute sour milk for* buttermilk *in the recipes in this book.*

To make sour milk:

Add 1 tablespoon of lemon juice to every cup of milk and let the milk sit for 15 minutes before adding it to the recipe.

Cream cheese

Be sure to use fresh cream cheese that does not have gum added as a preservative. Cheesecakes made with fresh cream cheese have a creamier and smoother consistency.

Mascarpone

Originating in Italy, mascarpone is now made by some American companies. (Italian mascarpone is also available in the United States.) Brands of mascarpone vary greatly from company to company. Mascarpone should be thick and smooth in consistency, and should not taste sour. It can be found in large grocery store chains or cheese shops. To make your own mascarpone, see page 254.

Eggs

At Stars we use Grade AA Large eggs for all our baking. Let the eggs you are going to use in the recipes sit at room temperature for 30 minutes before using them. Eggs at room temperature whip to a greater volume than refrigerated eggs.

Flour

We use all-purpose flour in all our recipes unless otherwise stated. Cake flour is made from soft wheat. It produces a cake with a finer crumb than one made with all-purpose flour. I often use half cake flour and half all-purpose flour in cake recipes. Tapioca flour is great for crisps and pie fillings because it thickens fruit mixtures quickly and pro- *duces a translucent sauce. It is available in oriental markets. If you cannot locate it, you can substitute 1 tablespoon all-purpose flour for each 1½ teaspoons tapioca flour.*

Nuts

Nuts have a high oil content and can go rancid easily. Always buy nuts in small quantities, preferably just for immediate use. If possible, buy them from places that sell them in bulk so you can taste them before you buy.

To toast nuts:

Preheat the oven to 325 degrees. Spread the nuts on a baking sheet in a single layer. Toast them for 10 minutes. Always toast nuts before using them in baking. Toasting them brings out their flavor and prevents them from becoming soggy when mixed with liquids in a dessert.

To chop nuts:

Always chop nuts by hand if you want them roughly or coarsely chopped. A food processor will overchop them very quickly. To grind nuts finely use a food processor and quick on and off turns. This will guarantee that they are ground evenly. Nuts with high oil content, such as pistachios or walnuts, are best ground with a little sugar or flour.

Salt

People are often surprised that salt is called for so frequently in baking. It is used in baking for the same reason it is used in all cooking—to bring out the flavors of the ingredients. The addition of just a pinch of salt can enhance the taste of desserts.

Spices

You can use spices already ground or grind your own for optimal flavor. In any event, be sure to buy spices that are full of aroma and bright in color. If possible, buy them from specialty food houses, where they are more apt to be of good quality.

Sweeteners

In all the recipes in the book, wherever sugar is specified, use granulated sugar unless otherwise instructed. Brown sugar is less refined than granulated sugar. Light and dark varieties are available. They both contain molasses, with dark brown sugar being treated with a darker grade molasses. Superfine sugar is a very fine crystallized white sugar. It dissolves quickly and is recommended for brûlées and in cold drinks. Be sure to buy the best quality of maple syrup that you can find. The best grades are light in color.

Vanilla and Almond Extract

Always buy vanilla in specialty cookware shops or food shops. There are many varieties of extracts and beans. Buy only pure extracts, not imitation. Madagascar produces excellent quality vanilla, and bourbon vanilla from Tahiti is another good variety. (It does not contain bourbon, but gets its name from the Bourbon Islands.) After whole vanilla beans are used, dry them off and immerse them in sugar in a sealed container. After several weeks, the sugar will pick up the vanilla flavor and can be used when you want the addition of vanilla flavoring. Use only very good quality pure almond extract. Imitation flavors have more of an alcohol taste than an almond flavor.

Equipment:
Scale

If you do not already have a scale, invest in one. They do not have to be expensive, and they are crucial for accurate weighing of butter, chocolate, and nuts.

Parchment Paper

When baking cakes, I prefer parchment paper to buttering and flouring the pans. Flour leaves a residue on the cake after it is baked. Parchment paper is also easier when baking cookies, as you do not have to keep buttering the baking sheets for each batch you bake. It is available in most grocery stores and cookware shops. When using parchment paper on baking sheets in a convection oven be sure to weight down the ends of the paper.

Ovens

Ovens are not identical in temperature. Therefore, treat the baking times given in the recipes in this book as approximate times. Check the dessert a couple of minutes before the specified time to be on the safe side. You can always leave it in the oven for a few minutes more.

Electric Mixers

Many of the recipes in this book can be prepared without an electric mixer. But if you do a lot of baking, an electric mixer is a good investment. Be sure to get one that has a heavy motor and comes with paddle, whisk, and dough attachments. Kenwood and KitchenAid are two reliable companies.

Mail Order Sources for
Baking Ingredients and Equipment

1. G. B. Ratto, International Grocers
   821 Washington Street
   Oakland, CA 94607
   Spices, extracts, chocolate, nuts and
   French Butter (delivered by overnight air).
   Write for catalogue.

2. American Spoon Foods
   411 East Lake Street
   Petoskey, MI 48235
   Dried sour cherries, maple syrups,
   dried wild blueberries, nuts and jams.
   Catalogue available.

3. Maid of Scandinavia
   3244 Raleigh Avenue
   Minneapolis, MN 55416
   Baking supplies and ingredients.
   Write for catalogue.

4. Williams Sonoma
   P.O. Box 7456
   San Francisco, CA 94120
   Baking equipment (savarin molds, ramekins,
   madeleine pans, steamed pudding molds) and
   gadgets you cannot live without, once you
   know that they exist. High-quality chocolate
   and vanilla beans and extract.
   Catalogue available.
   The store may have a branch.

Acknowledgments

*Hollyce Snyder for her invaluable personal and professional
assistance in the creation of this book.*

*Julia Orenstein for her support and assistance
in the editing of the recipes.*

*Jeremiah Tower and Mark Franz
for their professional support.*

*The staff of Stars and Stars Café
for continually promoting Stars' desserts.*

*Kyra Subbotin of the law firm
Rogers, Joseph, O'Donnell and Quinn.*

Recipe Testers:
*Mimi Csolti, Phyliss Crowley, Louise Franz, Mary Franz,
Chris Lasack, Katie Luchetti,
Scott Nelson, Lee Ann Powell, Ann Schnorbus,
and Emily Underhill*

Props:
Fillamento; San Francisco, California
Susan Fischer King; San Francisco, California
Paul Bauer; San Francisco, California

Index